Abingdon's Bible Zone LIVE

Where the Bible Comes to Life
In the Garden

Younger Elementary

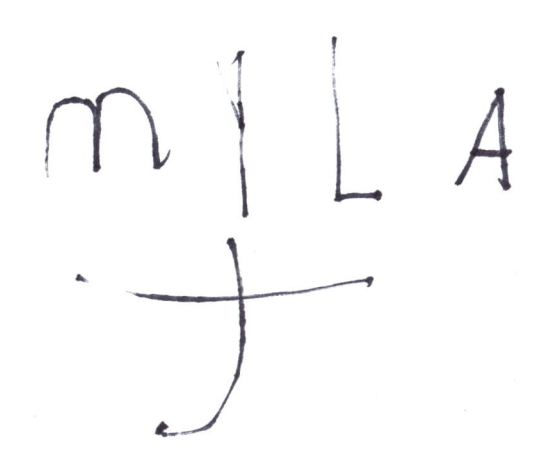

Also available from Abingdon Press:

Abingdon's BibleZone® LIVE
Preschool
FUNspirational® Kit

Abingdon's BibleZone® LIVE
Older Elementary
FUNspirational® Kit

Writer: Betsi H. Smith
Editor: Sally Wizik Wills
Production Editor: Sally Graham
Production and Design Manager:
R.E. Osborne
Designer: Paige Easter
Front Cover Photo: Ron Benedict
Back Cover Photo: Ron Benedict
Illustrator: Megan Jeffery

Abingdon's
BibleZONE LIVE
Younger Elementary

Where the Bible Comes to Life

IN THE GARDEN

Abingdon Press
Nashville

Abingdon's
BibleZone® LIVE
Where the Bible Comes to Life
In The Garden
Younger Elementary

Copyright © 2003 Abingdon Press

All rights reserved.

No part of this work, EXCEPT PATTERNS AND PAGES COVERED BY THE NOTICE BELOW, may be reproduced or transmitted in any form or by any means, electronic or mechanical, including photocopying and recording, or by any information storage or retrieval system, except as may be expressly permitted by the 1976 Copyright Act or by permission in writing from the publisher. Requests for permission should be submitted in writing to: Abingdon Press, 201 Eighth Avenue South, Nashville, TN 37203, faxed to (615) 749-6128, or submitted via email to *permission@abingdonpress.com*.

• NOTICE •
ONLY PATTERNS / PAGES that are marked **Reproducible** may be duplicated for use in the local church or church school. The following copyright notice is included on these pages and must appear on the reproduction:

Permission granted to photocopy for local church use. © 2003 Abingdon Press.

Unless otherwise noted, Scripture quotations are from the Contemporary English Version, © 1991, 1992, 1995 by the American Bible Society. Used by permission.

ISBN 0-687-09255-8

Art by Megan Jeffery.
Art p. 174 by Megan Jeffery © 1998 (Bible times man and woman), © 1999 (animals); pp. 74, 78 © 1999.
Art pp. 26, 30 by Robert S. Jones © 2003 Abingdon Press.

03 04 05 06 07 08 09 11 12 13—10 9 8 7 6 5 4 3 2 1

MANUFACTURED IN THE UNITED STATES OF AMERICA

Jesus is the Savior that God promised to send.

Scope the Zone

ZONE	TIME	SUPPLIES	ZILLIES
Zoom Into the Zone			
Arrival Time	10 minutes	Reproducible 1A, CD player, crayons or markers, pencils, nametags (page 170), tape or paper punch and yarn	CD
BibleZone			
Make Palm Branches	10 minutes	Reproducible 1B, green crayons or markers, scissors, tape, stapler and staples; green construction paper or dowel sticks or rulers	none
Coat On, Coat Off	5 minutes	two coats, palm branches	none
A Happy Day	10 minutes	palm branches (optional: garden materials)	zoo animal finger puppet
Bible Verse Scramble	5 minutes	Bible, index cards, marker	basket
Sing and Celebrate	10 minutes	CD player, palm branches	CD, kazoos
LifeZone			
I Promise	5 minutes	none	vinyl animal print kick ball
Closing Time	5 minutes	Bible, CD player	CD

Zillies® are found in the **BibleZone® LIVE FUNspirational® Kit**.

YOUNGER ELEMENTARY: LESSON 1

Zoom Into the Zone

Choose one or more activities to catch your children's interest.

Supplies:
Reproducible 1A
CD player
crayons or markers
nametags (page 170)
pencils
tape or paper punch and yarn

Zillies®:
CD

Arrival Time

Have the **CD** playing as the children enter the classroom. If possible, greet each child at the door as he or she arrives. Get down so that you are on each child's eye level.

Say: Welcome to BibleZone Live, (child's name)**! This is the place where we get to know the Bible, and we'll have fun doing it.**

If the children do not know one another, have them wear nametags **(see page 170)**. Let the children decorate the nametags. Tape the nametags to each child's clothes. If you want to reuse the nametags, punch holes in the top corners of each nametag. Cut pieces of yarn long enough to fit over a child's head. Tie the yarn through the holes in the nametags.

Give the children the Palm Sunday maze (**Reproducible 1A**) that you photocopied before class. Have the children trace the path that Jesus would take through Jerusalem. Tell the children to copy down the letters they pass and to use them to fill in the blanks below.

Ask: What do the letters spell? (Palm Sunday) **That's right. Today we're going to talk about Palm Sunday.**

Teacher Tip: If your church is in a location where you can take the children outside, plan to spend some of your class time out of doors this quarter. Arrange for extra adult supervision, if necessary.

**Jesus is the Savior
that God promised to send.**

Bible Zone

Choose one or more activities to immerse your children in the Bible story.

Make Palm Branches

Supplies:
Reproducible 1B
green crayons or markers
scissors
tape
stapler and staples
green construction paper, dowel sticks, or rulers

Zillies®:
none

Before class, photocopy the palm branch (**Reproducible 1B**), one for each child.

Give each child a palm branch. Let the children use green crayons or markers to decorate their palms. Help the children cut out their palm branches.

Give each child a piece of green construction paper. Show the children how to fold the paper accordion-style and wrap tape around it to create a sturdy stem for their palm branch. Have the children tape or staple the stem to their palm branches. *(Or let the children use dowel sticks or rulers for the stems.)* Let the children wave their palm branches.

Say: In today's Bible story the people were so happy that they waved palm branches.

Coat On, Coat Off

Supplies:
two coats
palm branches

Zillies®:
none

Divide the children into two teams. Have them line up on one side of the room. Have the children hold their palm branches. Place a chair on the other side of the room. Have a coat for each team at the starting point.

Say: When I say go, the first person on each team should put on your team's coat and run *(or walk quickly, if you prefer)* **to the other side of the room. When you reach the chair, you should take off the coat, lay it on the ground, and wave your palm branch and say "Hosanna!" Then you should put the coat back on and come back to the starting point. When you tag the next person in line, that person will do the same thing, until everyone on the team has completed the relay.**

Play until both teams finish. Keep the competition friendly.

Say: In our Bible story today, the people were so happy, they did what you just did—they laid their coats on the ground. They waved palm branches and shouted "Hosanna!" Let's find out why they were so happy.

YOUNGER ELEMENTARY: LESSON 1

Bible Zone Story

A Happy Day

By Betsi H. Smith

> Since many of this quarter's Bible stories take place in a garden, turn your storytelling area into a garden. Gather and arrange a variety of greenery, either real, silk, or a combination of both. If you know someone who owns a garden shop, borrow plants. *(Let the children help care for the plants; it teaches responsibility for the world.)* Bring in a small water fountain, as well as a sound machine. *(These small machines, often found in electronics departments at discount stores, may let you change the sounds so that the children can listen to waves, birds, rain, and so forth.)*
>
> You will begin and end storytime all quarter with a **zoo animal finger puppet**. Keep the puppet out of sight and bring it out only for storytime; the puppet will hold the children's interest longer; and the children will know as soon as they see the puppet that it is time to hear the Bible story.
>
> Have the children bring their palm branches to the story area. Put your index finger and middle finger into the puppet's front legs. Bring the puppet out to talk to the children. Create a name for the puppet, or let the children name it.

Have the puppet **say: Hello, everyone! My name is** *(puppet's name).* **What are your names?** *Have the children say their names.* **I'm a lucky** *(lion, zebra. and so forth)*, **because I get to visit with you the next few weeks. I love stories, especially stories from the Bible. Today's story is a happy story about Jesus and a time that we call Palm Sunday. I'd like you to help tell today's Bible story. When you hear your teacher say, "Jesus is coming!" wave your palm branches and say, "Hosanna! Blessed is the king who comes in the name of the Lord."** *(Let the children practice.)* **I'll just hang out and enjoy the story.** *(Set the puppet aside.)*

Jesus and his friends had been walking for a while. Finally, they could see the city of Jerusalem in the distance.

"See Jerusalem down there?" Jesus said, pointing to the city. "I want two of you to go there ahead of the rest of us. When you find a young colt tied up, bring it to me."

The two men went into the town, and as Jesus had said, they found a young colt tied up. When the two men started to leave with the colt, some people tried to stop them.

"You don't own that animal," someone said.

BibleZone® LIVE

"But the Lord needs it," one of Jesus' friends protested. So the people let them take the colt back to Jesus.

Before Jesus could climb on the colt, some of his friends took off their coats and laid them across the colt's back.

"My coat will cushion your ride," one of them said.

"My coat will keep you from getting dirty sitting on that colt's back," said another. Jesus sat on the colt. He pointed the colt in the direction of the city of Jerusalem, and off he went.

All along the way to Jerusalem, people started to talk. And this is what they said: "**Jesus is coming!**" *(Have the children wave their palm branches and say, "Hosanna! Blessed is the king who comes in the name of the Lord.")*

The people were happy to see Jesus riding into town. They had heard their whole lives that God was going to send a Savior, a king who would be kind and wise and who would save them from their enemies. Everyone had been waiting a long time for the Savior that God had promised. Now it was finally happening. **Jesus was coming!** *(Have the children wave their palm branches and say, "Hosanna! Blessed is the king who comes in the name of the Lord.")*

There was so much excitement in town that day! People cut down palm branches and waved them in the air. They spread branches out on the road in front of Jesus. They took off their coats and laid them on the path where that colt was going to walk. And the whole time, they were calling out to one another, "Can you believe it? Can you believe it? **Jesus is coming!**" *(Have the children wave their palm branches and say, "Hosanna! Blessed is the king who comes in the name of the Lord.")*

When Jesus passed by, he saw all the people waving at him. He could tell how happy they were to see him. He could tell that this was a happy day in Jerusalem.

"Hosanna!" everyone shouted. "Blessed is the king who comes in the name of the Lord. Hosanna! **Jesus is coming**!" *(Have the children wave their palm branches and say, "Hosanna! Blessed is the king who comes in the name of the Lord.")*

Bring the puppet back out to talk to the children.

Have the puppet say: I loved that story. I loved hearing about how happy everyone was to see Jesus.

Have the puppet ask: Can you guess why we call that day Palm Sunday? *(because people waved palm branches)* **And why do you think that everyone was so happy to see Jesus?** *(Jesus was the Savior for whom they had been waiting their whole lives.)* **Can I hear you say that phrase one more time, the one you said whenever your teacher said, "Jesus is coming!"?** *(Have the children say, "Hosanna! Blessed is the king who comes in the name of the Lord.")* **Thank you! That makes me very happy.**

Have the puppet say goodbye until next week.

BibleZone

Choose one or more activities to immerse your children in the Bible story.

Supplies:
Bible
index cards
marker

Zillies®:
basket

Bible Verse Scramble

Before class, write the Bible verse on index cards, dividing it into sections: "Blessed is the king / who comes in the name / of the Lord." Put one section on each card so that you have three cards per verse. Make duplicate sets, since you will need one card per student.

Have a student hold the Bible open to Luke. Show the children where today's verse is found in the Bible. Say the Bible verse for the students. Have them repeat it. Remind them that this is the phrase they just finished repeating in the Bible story.

Fold the Bible verse cards and put them in a **basket**, making sure you have one card per student and that you have the correct cards to form the Bible verse in its entirety. If the number of students in your class cannot be divided evenly by three, include a card for yourself or have two students share a card.

Have the students come one at a time and draw a card from the basket.

Say: That card you're holding is part of today's Bible verse. Call out your part of the Bible verse and find the people who have the rest of the Bible verse. You each need two other people. When you find them, stand so that the Bible verse is in order.

**Jesus is the Savior
that God promised to send.**

16

BibleZone® LIVE

Life Zone

Choose one or more activities to bring the Bible to life.

Sing and Celebrate

Gather the children. Have them bring their palm branches with them. Play the song "Hosanna, Hallelujah!" **(CD, Track 2)**. Let the children listen to the song once. Play it again and encourage the children to sing along (see the words on page 17). Give each child a **kazoo**.

Say: When people want to celebrate something that makes them happy, they have a parade. The people were happy on Palm Sunday because God had sent the Savior that God had promised to send. Let's have a parade to celebrate Palm Sunday.

Play "Hosanna, Hallelujah!" again and lead the children in a parade. Encourage the children to play the kazoos and to wave their palm branches as they march. Wind the parade between tables and chairs and all around your classroom. (At the end, collect the kazoos. Wash them in warm, soapy water before they are used again.)

Supplies:
CD player
palm branches

Zillies®:
CD
kazoos

Hosanna, Hallelujah!

Refrain:
Hosanna, hallelujah!
Sing we loud and clear.
Hosanna, hallelujah!
Jesus Christ is near.
With ancient psalms
and new grown palms,
praise him on his way.
Hosanna, Hallelujah!
Christ, our Lord, is here.

This day in spring the streets will ring
with voices sweet and lyrical
to greet our Lord, the one adored,
his very life a miracle.

Refrain

King David's Son now rides upon
a mule of beasts the lowliest
amidst the throng it bears along of
humankind the holiest.

Refrain

How very odd the Son of God must
do things that would weary us.
God will amaze; God works in
ways that we all find mysterious.

Refrain

WORDS and MUSIC: Richard K. Avery and Donald S. Marsh.
Words and music copyright © 1967 by Richard K. Avery and Donald S. Marsh.
Used by permission of Hope Publishing Co., Carol Stream, IL 60187

YOUNGER ELEMENTARY: LESSON 1

Life Zone

Choose one or more activities to bring the Bible to life.

Supplies:
none

Zillies®:
vinyl animal print kick ball

I Promise

Gather the children in a circle. Have a **vinyl animal print kick ball** with you.

Say: God promised the world a Savior, and God kept that promise. When we make promises, it's important that we keep our promises too.

Have the children think about a promise that they can keep next week.

Ask: Is there someone in your family to whom you can be nicer? You can promise to do that next week. Is there a chore that your mom or dad has to remind you to do? You can promise to do that next week without being asked. Is there someone new at school who hasn't made many friends? You can promise to be nice to that person next week. *(Hold up the animal print ball.)* **We'll pass the ball around the circle. When you get the ball, say "I promise . . ." and tell us what you promise to do next week.**

Start by making a promise yourself. Pass the ball to the child on your left. Encourage, but do not force, each child to participate.

Supplies:
Bible
CD player

Zillies®:
CD

Closing Time

Play "Morning Has Broken" **(CD, Track 12)** to signal the children that it is closing time. **Say the Bible verse for the children: "Blessed is the king who comes in the name of the Lord"** (Luke 19:38). Have the children repeat it.

Say: Remember that Palm Sunday was a happy time because God had sent Jesus, who was the Savior that God had promised. Remember the promise that you made for next week.

Pray: God, thank you for Jesus. We're so happy that you kept your promise to us to send the world a Savior. Help us to keep the promises we made next week. Amen.

Have the children take home their palm branches and coats.

Give each child a copy of HomeZone® to take home to parents.

Home Zone For Parents

Bible Verse
Blessed is the king who comes in the name of the Lord!
Luke 19:38

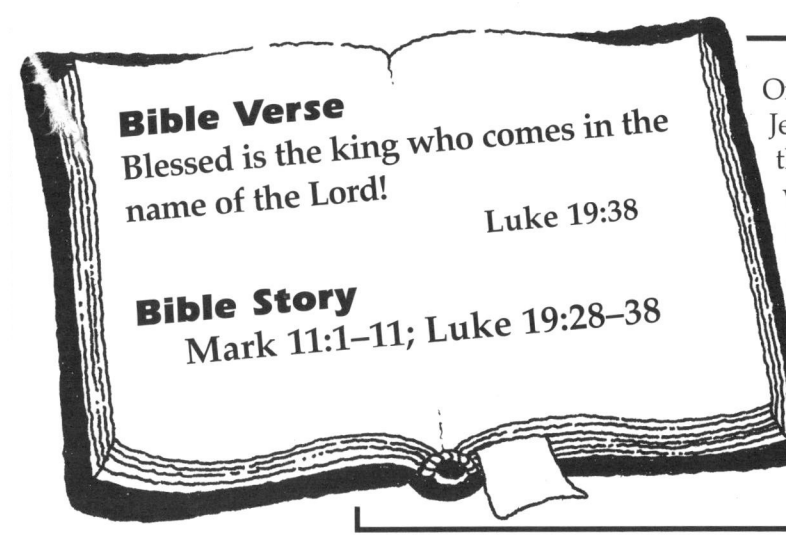

Bible Story
Mark 11:1–11; Luke 19:28–38

On Palm Sunday, Jesus rode a colt into Jerusalem. People welcomed him by spreading their cloaks on the road in front of him. They waved palm branches and called out "Hosanna!", which means "Save us!", as Jesus passed by. Has your child ever seen a parade? If so, talk with your child about his or her memories of that day. Were people smiling? Were they cheering? Was there a happy feeling? Tell your child that the people who welcomed Jesus on that Palm Sunday long ago felt many of the same feelings.

Same Letters, New Words

Take turns with your child thinking of phrases that begin with the same letters that begin the words *Palm Sunday* (*pretty snake, puffy shoes*). Or have your child think of a word that starts with the letter *P*, while you finish the phrase by adding a word that starts with the letter *S*.

Chocolate-Coated Pretzels

You will need: chocolate chips, twist pretzels, forks, and wax paper. Candy sprinkles are optional.

For a snack that looks fancy and tastes great, dip pretzels in chocolate. Melt ½ cup chocolate chips in a microwave oven. Let your child stir the chocolate every 30 seconds until the chocolate is melted. Let your child drop a pretzel into the melted chocolate and use a fork to turn the pretzel to make sure both sides are thoroughly coated. Again using a fork, lift each pretzel out of the chocolate and lay it on wax paper until the chocolate hardens. Coat one pretzel at a time. If you like, before the chocolate hardens, top the pretzels with candy sprinkles.

Jesus is the Savior that God promised to send.

YOUNGER ELEMENTARY: LESSON 1   Permission granted to photocopy for local church use. © 2003 Abingdon Press.

Reproducible 1A

Permission granted to photocopy for local church use. © 2003 Abingdon Press.

BibleZone® L1

ZONE IN

When we celebrate Communion, we remember Jesus.

Scope the Zone

ZONE	TIME	SUPPLIES	ZILLIES
Zoom Into the Zone			
Arrival Time	10 minutes	Reproducible 2A, CD player, crayons or markers, nametags (page 170), tape or paper punch and yarn, scissors	CD
What's Different?	5 minutes	glue, scissors, crayons, bath towel or piece of fabric	vinyl animal print kick ball, basket, duster pen, mini flashlight keychain, smile face missle ball, animal world beach ball, kazoo, magnifying glass
BibleZone			
Make a Time Capsule	10 minutes	Reproducible 2B, crayons or markers, cardboard tubes, gift wrap, scissors, tape	none
Remember Me	10 minutes	optional: garden materials	zoo animal finger puppet
Shrinking Circles	5 minutes	Bible, yarn, scissors	none
Bread and Juice	5 minutes	crackers or uncut loaf of bread, napkins, grape juice, small cups	none
Sing and Celebrate	5 minutes	CD player	CD
LifeZone			
I Remember . . .	5 minutes	none	smile face missile ball
Closing Time	5 minutes	CD player	CD

Zillies® are found in the **BibleZone® LIVE FUNspirational® Kit.**

YOUNGER ELEMENTARY: LESSON 2

23

Zoom Into the Zone

Choose one or more activities to catch your children's interest.

Supplies:
Reproducible 2A
CD player
crayons or markers
nametags (page 170)
tape or paper punch and yarn
scissors

Zillies®:
CD

Arrival Time

Before class, photocopy and cut apart the Communion matching cards **(Reproducible 2A)**. You will need two sets for every child.

Have the **CD** playing as the children enter the classroom. If possible, greet each child at the door as he or she arrives. Make eye contact with each child, getting down on the child's level, if possible.

Say: Welcome to BibleZone Live, *(child's name)*! **This is the place where we get to know the Bible, and we'll have fun doing it. I'm glad you're here today.**

If the children do not know one another, have them wear nametags again this week **(see page 170)**. Let any new children decorate their nametags.

Give the children the Communion matching cards. Have the children match the cards. Tell the children that the cards show different things that people use to celebrate the Lord's Supper. If you have time, let the children use markers or crayons to decorate their matching cards.

Supplies:
glue
scissors
crayons
bath towel or piece of fabric

Zillies®:
vinyl animal print kick ball
basket
duster pen
mini flashlight keychain
smile face missle ball
animal world beach ball
kazoo
magnifying glass

What's Different?

Have a variety of Zillies on hand, along with some simple classroom supplies such as a bottle of glue, scissors, and a box of crayons. Arrange the items on a table. Have a bath towel or a piece of cloth big enough to completely cover the arrangement.

Show the children the objects. Review the name of each one.

Have the children turn their backs. Remove one item. Let the children try to guess what is missing. Or rearrange the items, and let the children try to guess what has been moved.

Say: You did a good job remembering what was on the table. Jesus wanted his friends to remember him when he was gone, so he told them a special way to remember him. We'll hear more about that in our Bible story today.

Bible Zone

Choose one or more activities to immerse your children in the Bible story.

Make a Time Capsule

Say: Sometimes when people want to remember a special day, they will make something called a time capsule. They will pick objects that they want to include. They will put these items in a container, and they will put that container away for a long time. When they finally open the time capsule, the items they put in it will help them remember the special day. Let's make our own time capsules.

Give the children the information sheet (**Reproducible 2B**) that you photocopied before class.

Have the children fill out the information sheet. Provide any needed reading and writing assistance. Let the children use crayons or markers to color the border on their information sheets.

Give each child a cardboard tube cut into sections. Have the children roll up their information sheets and put them inside the tubes. Let the children cover their cardboard tubes in wrapping paper or tissue paper, folding over and taping shut both ends.

Tape a strip of masking tape on each time capsule. Help the children decide when they want to open their time capsules. Write the date on each time capsule.

Supplies:
Reproducible 2B
crayons or markers
cardboard tubes
gift wrap
scissors
tape

Zillies®:
none

> **Zone In:** When we celebrate Communion, we remember Jesus.

YOUNGER ELEMENTARY: LESSON 2

25

Bible Zone Story

Remember Me

By Betsi H. Smith

> See Lesson 1 *(page 14)* for suggestions on how to turn your storytelling area into a garden.
>
> Bring out the **zoo animal finger puppet**. Put your index finger and third finger into the puppet's front legs.

Have the puppet **say: Remember me? My name is** *(puppet's name)*. **Can you tell me your names again?** *(Have the children say their names.)* **I'm glad to see all of you. I'm a lucky animal, because I get to chill with you for the next few weeks. I love Bible stories. In this week's story, Jesus wanted his friends to always think of him, so he came up with a way to help them remember him. Can I hang around and listen to the story? Thanks!** *(Set the puppet aside for now.)*

Show the children how to say the Bible verse, "Remember me," in American sign language. Tell them that when you signal them, you want them to say and sign "Remember me."

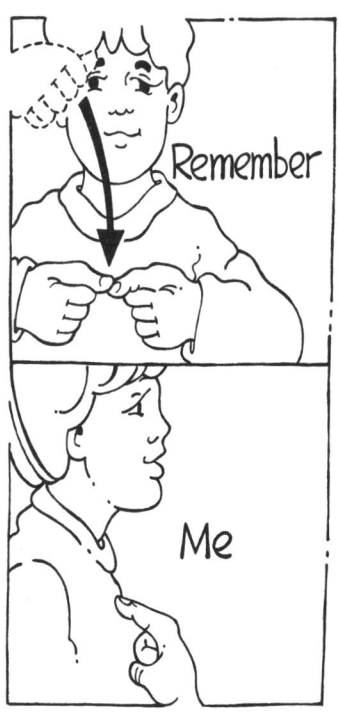

Jesus sat back and looked around him. It was a special time of year, a time called Passover. Jesus was celebrating the Passover with his twelve special friends, his disciples.

Jesus loved the twelve disciples. Oh, he knew that sometimes they didn't understand what he was trying to tell them. And sometimes they fought with one another about silly things, like who got to sit beside Jesus or who was the most important. But they were good men. Most of them had given up a lot to follow him, and Jesus knew that they loved him as much as he loved them.

Earlier that day, the disciples had come to Jesus and asked him what to do to get ready for the evening meal. Jesus sent them into the city to ask a man who lived there if they could all eat at his house that night. The man said yes, and now here they were, enjoying this special meal.

Jesus chewed slowly on a piece of bread while he listened to the disciples talking around him. He enjoyed being with them, especially for the Passover meal, but he was a little sad too. See, Jesus knew something that they didn't know. He knew that this would be the last meal that he would eat with all of his disciples. God had other plans for Jesus, and those plans were going to start happening very soon.

"I don't want my friends to forget me when I'm gone," Jesus thought to himself. "I've spent so much time with them, teaching them about God's love and about how God wants them to live. I want them to remember all that I've taught them. I want them to remember me."
Response:
"Remember me," Jesus said.
(Have the children sign "Remember me.")
"Remember what I said and did.
I will always remember you,
so please remember me."
(Have the children sign "Remember me.")

Jesus knew what to do. He got everyone's attention. Then he picked up a loaf of bread. He said a blessing over the bread, and he broke it in half. Jesus handed the bread to his disciples and told them to eat it.

"Whenever you eat bread, remember that I love you," Jesus said. "I want you to remember me."

(Repeat the response.)

Then Jesus took a cup of juice. He thanked God for the juice and then he gave it to his disciples and told them to drink it.

"Whenever you drink juice, remember the things I told you," Jesus said. "I want you to remember me."

(Repeat the response.)

Bring the puppet back out to talk to the children.

Have the puppet say: That was a good idea that Jesus had. We all have to eat, right? If we remember Jesus whenever we eat and drink, we'll be remembering Jesus all the time. Our church even has a special time when we celebrate this last meal that Jesus ate with his disciples. We call it the Lord's Supper. *(Change the name to the* Last Supper *or to* Holy Communion, *depending on how your church refers to the sacrament.)* **I liked that verse you were saying and the sign language you did with it. If I had fingers instead of** *(hooves, paws, and so forth)*, **I could sign "Remember me" too. Will you show it to me again?** *(Have the children sign "Remember me.")* **Thanks! I appreciate it.**

Have the puppet say goodbye until next week.

YOUNGER ELEMENTARY: LESSON 2

Bible Zone

Choose one or more activities to immerse your children in the Bible story.

Supplies:
Bible
yarn
scissors

Zillies®:
none

Shrinking Circles

Before class, cut pieces of yarn five feet long to make circles. You will need one circle per child. Tie the ends of each circle together.

Have a student hold the Bible open to 1 Corinthians. Show the children where today's verse is found in the Bible. **Say the Bible verse for the students: "Remember me"** (1 Corinthians 11:24). Have them repeat it.

Gather the children in an open area of the room. Spread the circles out on the floor. Have each child stand in a separate circle.

Say: Let's have fun with the Bible verse. I will start out saying the Bible verse—"Remember me"—but sometimes instead of saying it correctly, I'll say it wrong. When I say it wrong, don't move. When I say it right, move to a different circle. But there is a catch: Each time you move, I will take away one circle. That means some of you will have to share a circle. By the end, there will only be one circle left, and all of you will try to have one foot inside the circle.

Start each time by saying the first word, "Remember" but change the second word (*pizza, puppies, snow, belly buttons, butterflies, tractors, mittens, and so forth*). Every third or fourth time, say the Bible verse correctly.

Supplies:
crackers or uncut
   loaf of bread
napkins
grape juice
small cups

Zillies®:
none

Bread and Juice

Have the children gather at a table. Have crackers or an uncut loaf of bread on the table, as well as a pitcher of grape juice and small cups. Have a child hand out napkins. Give each child a cracker or a small piece of bread. Have a child pass out the cups of juice as you fill them. Let the children enjoy their bread or crackers and grape juice.

Say: Jesus gave his friends a special way to remember him. He chose bread and grape juice because he wanted us to remember him whenever we ate a meal.

Teacher Tip: If possible, have your pastor or Communion steward talk to your children about Communion. Or take your children to the sanctuary so they can see where Communion takes place.

BibleZone® LIVE

Life Zone

Choose one or more activities to bring the Bible to life.

Sing and Celebrate

Lead the children in singing the song "Hosanna, Hallelujah!" **(CD, Track 2)**. Remind them that the people waved palm branches and shouted "Hosanna!" as Jesus rode into Jerusalem.

Supplies:
CD player

Zillies®:
CD

Hosanna, Hallelujah!

Refrain:
Hosanna, hallelujah!
Sing we loud and clear.
Hosanna, hallelujah!
Jesus Christ is near.
With ancient psalms
and new grown palms,
praise him on his way.
Hosanna, Hallelujah!
Christ, our Lord, is here.

This day in spring the streets will ring
with voices sweet and lyrical
to greet our Lord, the one adored,
his very life a miracle.

Refrain

King David's Son now rides upon
a mule of beasts the lowliest
amidst the throng it bears along of
humankind the holiest.

Refrain

How very odd the Son of God must
do things that would weary us.
God will amaze; God works in
ways that we all find mysterious.

Refrain

WORDS and MUSIC: Richard K. Avery and Donald S. Marsh
Words and music copyright © 1967 by Richard K. Avery and Donald S. Marsh.
Used by permission of Hope Publishing Co., Carol Stream, IL 60187.

YOUNGER ELEMENTARY: LESSON 2

Life Zone

Choose one or more activities to bring the Bible to life.

Supplies:
none

Zillies®:
smile face missile ball

I Remember . . .

Have the children stand in a circle. Hold up one of the **smile face missile balls**.

Say: Think of something you remember about Jesus. When you think of something, raise your hand. I'll throw you the ball. Tell us what you remember, then throw the ball back to me.

Give the children suggestions, if necessary, such as Jesus was born in a manger; Jesus is the Son of God; Mary was Jesus' mother; Jesus healed people.

Say: Jesus wanted his friends to remember him when he was gone, so he told them a special way to remember him.

Supplies:
CD player

Zillies®:
CD

Closing Time

Play "Morning Has Broken" (**CD, Track 12**) to signal the children that it is closing time. **Say the Bible verse: "Remember me"** (1 Corinthians 11:24). Have the children repeat it and say the verse in American sign language.

Have the children hold hands.

Pray: God, thank you for giving us your Son, Jesus. Help us remember Jesus and all the things that he has done for us. We want to remember Jesus whenever we eat bread and drink juice. Amen.

Have the children take home their time capsules.

Give each child a copy of the HomeZone to take home to parents.

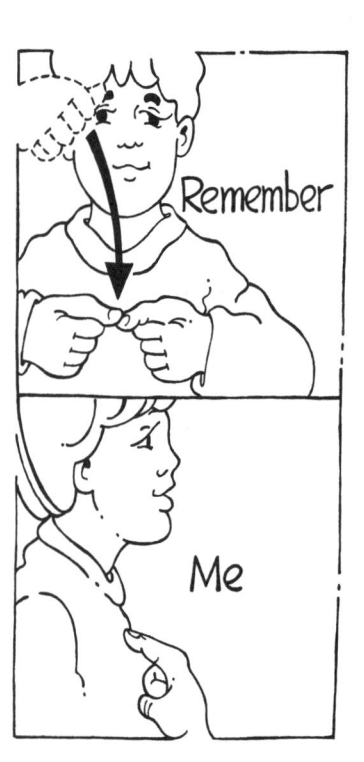

Home Zone For Parents

Bible Verse
Remember me.
1 Corinthians 11:24

Bible Story
Matthew 26:17–30; Luke 22:7–23

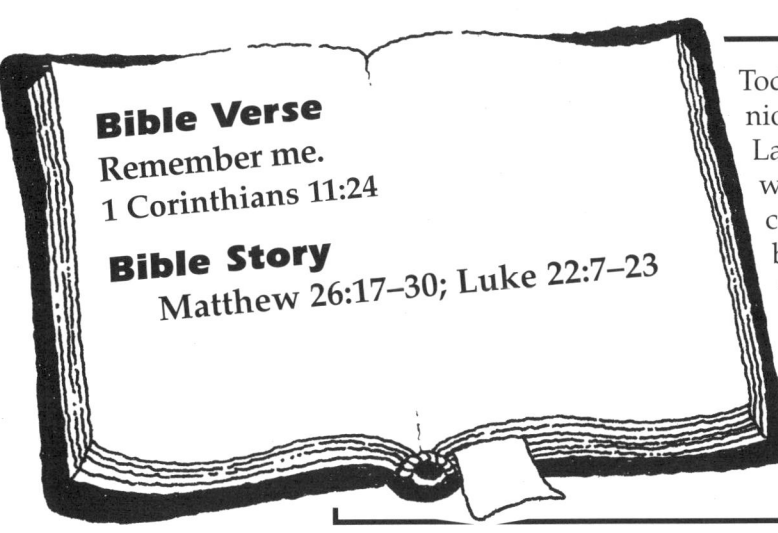

Today your child learned about Holy Communion, also known as the Lord's Supper or the Last Supper. Talk about Holy Communion with your child, but since young children are concrete thinkers, avoid talking about the body and the blood of Christ. Your child will not grasp the symbolism. Instead, emphasize that Jesus wanted his followers to have a special way to remember him. Tell your child that when we eat bread and drink juice during the Lord's Supper, we do so to remember Jesus.

Faces to Remember

Sit facing your child. Make a funny face. Encourage your child to copy your expression and then to add a second funny face. Copy both expressions and add a third. Play as long as you can remember the expressions. Start over when one of you loses your place. Remind your child that Jesus gave us a special way to remember him.

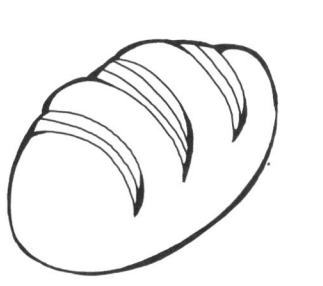

Cheesy Popcorn

You will need: a bag of microwave popcorn and cheese spread.

Pop a bag of popcorn, according to the directions on the package. Dump the popcorn in a large bowl. (Careful! When you open the bag, the steam will be hot.) In a microwave-safe bowl, melt 1 cup cheese spread. Let your child stir the cheese every 20 seconds until it is melted. Take the cheese out of the microwave. Pour the melted cheese on top of the popcorn. Let your child use a large spoon to stir the two together. Let cool and eat!

When we celebrate Communion, we remember Jesus.

YOUNGER ELEMENTARY: LESSON 2   Permission granted to photocopy for local church use. © 2003 Abingdon Press.

Reproducible 2A

Permission granted to photocopy for local church use. © 2003 Abingdon Press.

BibleZone® LIVE

My name is _____

I am _____ years old.

My favorite food is _____.

My favorite movie is _____.

My favorite television show is
_____

My favorite color is _____.

My best friends are _____.

My favorite Bible story is
_____

In school I like to _____.

When I grow up, I want to be a
_____.

YOUNGER ELEMENTARY: LESSON 2

Reproducible 2B

Permission granted to photocopy for local church use. © 2003 Abingdon Press.

3 BibleZone LIVE

Watch With Me

Enter the Zone

Bible Verse
You want to do what is right, but you are weak.
> Mark 14:38

Bible Story
Matthew 26:36-46; Mark 14:32-42

Following the Last Supper, Jesus and his disciples walked to the garden of Gethsemane. Jesus took Peter, James, and John farther into the garden. Jesus admitted to these three men how distraught he was over the events that were about to take place. He asked them to stay awake and keep him company. Then Jesus went a little farther and fell face down on the ground, asking God to spare him from the upcoming ordeal. Instead of staying awake, Peter, James, and John fell asleep. Jesus woke them and asked them to pray. But a second time, and then a third time, the disciples fell asleep.

How could the disciples have let Jesus down, not once, not even twice, but three times? It's simple; Jesus said it himself when he woke them up the first time: The spirit is willing, but the flesh is weak (Matthew 26:41). How often do you begin your devotional time, only to find your mind wandering? Who among us has fallen asleep while saying our evening prayers?

The good news is that Jesus loves us anyway, in spite of our weaknesses.
The image of Jesus lying on the ground, begging God to release him from his fate, is heartbreaking. During your darkest moments, have you ever wondered if anyone can understand your pain? Picture Jesus in the garden and know that he felt loneliness and heartache on a level that we cannot even comprehend. Jesus understands, because Jesus lived it.

The children you teach may have already experienced some of the same feelings that Jesus felt. They can know sadness, grief, betrayal, and fear of the future. Take special note of any children in your class who are going through a difficult time. Model Jesus' love for them. Help them understand that God is always there for them, in good times and in bad times.

ZONE IN

God is with us when we have difficult things to do.

Scope the Zone

ZONE	TIME	SUPPLIES	ZILLIES®
Zoom Into the Zone			
Arrival Time	10 minutes	Reproducible 3A, CD player, pencils, nametags (page 170), tape or paper punch and yarn	CD
All Tied Up	5 minutes	none	none
BibleZone®			
Write the Wrong Way	5 minutes	paper, tape, yardstick	duster pen
Make Sleepy Faces	10 minutes	Reproducible 3B, yarn, utility knife, scissors, plain paper plates, pencil, crayons or markers, glue, ruler	none
Jesus' Sleepy Friends	10 minutes	sleepy faces	zoo animal finger puppet
Bible Verse Toss-up	10 minutes	Bible	animal world beach ball
Which Is Harder?	10 minutes	none	none
LifeZone			
Sing and Celebrate	5 minutes	CD player	CD
Mosaic Wall Hanging	5 minutes	Reproducible 3B, scissors, crayons or markers, glue, tape, yarn or ribbon (optional: instant-developing camera and film	colored foam squares
Closing Time	5 minutes	CD player	CD, bird warblers

Zillies® are found in the **BibleZone® LIVE FUNspirational® Kit.**

YOUNGER ELEMENTARY: LESSON 3

35

Zoom Into the Zone

Choose one or more activities to catch your children's interest.

Supplies:
Reproducible 3A
CD player
pencils
nametags (page 170)
tape or paper punch and yarn

Zillies®:
CD

Arrival Time

Have the **CD** playing as the children enter the classroom. If possible, greet each child at the door as he or she arrives. Make eye contact with each child, getting down on the child's level, if possible.

Say: Welcome to BibleZone Live, *(child's name)*! **This is the place where we get to know the Bible, and we'll have fun doing it. I'm glad you're here today.**

If the children do not know one another, encourage them to wear nametags again this week **(see page 170)**.

Give the children the picture of Jesus praying in the garden **(Reproducible 3A)** that you photocopied before class. Encourage the children to find and circle four things in the picture that don't belong.

Supplies:
none

Zillies®:
none

All Tied Up

Divide the children into groups of four or five. Have each group stand in a close circle. Have each child stretch out his or her left hand toward the center and hold onto someone else's left hand. Have each child stretch out his or her right hand toward the center and hold onto someone else's right hand.

Tell the children to try to untangle their arms without letting go of one another's hands. Let them have fun trying, but watch for children who might pull too hard in their eagerness to accomplish this task.

Say: That was hard, wasn't it? In today's Bible story, Jesus' disciples had a hard time doing something that Jesus wanted them to do.

> **God is with us when we have difficult things to do.**

BibleZone® LIVE

Bible Zone

Choose one or more activities to immerse your children in the Bible story.

Write the Wrong Way

Before class, tape one of the **duster pens** securely to the end of a yardstick. Remove the base (the feet).

Say: Let's try something else that's hard to do.

Hand one of the children the duster pen that is not taped to a yardstick. Place a piece of paper on the floor at the child's feet. Tell the child to kneel down and write his or her name anywhere on the paper.

Ask: Good job! Was that hard or easy? *(easy)*

Now have the child put the edge of his or her foot on each side to hold the paper in place. Hand the child the pen that is taped to the yardstick. Tell the child to write his or her name again, this time standing up straight and using the longer pen.

Ask: Was that hard or easy? *(hard)* **Jesus' disciples had to do something that was hard. In a minute we'll hear what that was.**

Let the children take turns writing their names with the longer pen.

Supplies:
paper
tape
yardstick

Zillies®:
duster pen

Make Sleepy Faces

Before class, cut yarn into short pieces. Prepare plain white paper plates (not plastic foam) for the craft activity by cutting slits for the eye strips **(Reproducible 3B)**. Lay a eye strip horizontally across the center of each paper plate. Using the strip as a guide, draw four vertical lines across the top of each plate. The lines should be two inches tall. Use scissors or a utility knife to cut the lines into slits. Photocopy **Reproducible 3B,** cutting the eye strips apart from the wall hanging. Set the wall hanging aside for now.

Have each child thread his or her eye strip through the slits in the paper plate. Let the children use crayons or markers to draw noses, mouths, and so forth on their faces. Let the children glue yarn on the faces to make hair and/or beards. Show the children how to make the eyes open and close by sliding the strips back and forth.

Supplies:
Reproducible 3B
yarn
utility knife
scissors
plain paper plates
pencil
crayons or markers
glue
ruler

Zillies®:
none

YOUNGER ELEMENTARY: LESSON 3

Bible Story

Jesus' Sleepy Friends

By Betsi H. Smith

> **Say: We'll use our sleepy faces to tell the Bible story today.**
>
> See Lesson 1 (page 14) for suggestions on how to turn your storytelling area into a garden. Have the children bring their sleepy faces to the storytelling area. Bring out the **zoo animal finger puppet.**

Have the puppet say: Remember me? My name is *(puppet's name)*. **It must be storytime again. Today I hear that you're going to use the sleepy faces that you just made to help tell the story. I can't wait to see that! Today's story is about a time when Jesus needed his friends, and they let him down. Can you imagine letting Jesus down? I've got to hear this story.** *(Set the puppet aside for now. Make sure the children have the eyes open on their sleepy faces.)*

It was nighttime in the garden of Gethsemane. Jesus had gone to the garden after he and the disciples had eaten the Passover Meal together.

"Come with me," Jesus said to his friends. "I want to pray."

Jesus stayed with his friends for a few minutes, but then he walked a little farther into the garden. He wanted to be by himself, but he wanted his friends close by.

"Stay right here," Jesus said. "Wait for me while I go over there and pray."

Jesus' friends wanted to do exactly what Jesus told them to do. But it had been a long day for them, and they had just eaten a big meal. It was so dark in the peaceful garden, and a nice, gentle breeze was rustling the leaves. Pretty soon their eyes started getting heavy, and then their heads started to drift over. Before they knew it, they were sound asleep.

(Have the children pull the strips on their sleepy faces to close the eyes.)

"Wake up!" Jesus said, shaking Peter's shoulder.

Peter and the other disciples jerked themselves awake.

(Have the children pull the strips on their sleepy faces to open the eyes.)

Couldn't you stay awake for even one hour?" Jesus asked Peter.

"We didn't mean to fall asleep," Peter said.

"I know you didn't, but you just weren't strong enough," Jesus said. "Please stay awake while I talk to God about a big decision. I need my friends to pray for me."

"We will, Jesus," his friends promised.

Jesus went back to where he was praying. Jesus' friends started to pray. They wanted to keep on praying, they really did—but they just couldn't keep their eyes open. Once again, they fell asleep.

(Have the children pull the strips on their sleepy faces to close the eyes.)

"Are you asleep again?" they heard Jesus say, and their eyes popped open.

(Have the children pull the strips on their sleepy faces to open the eyes.)

"We're sorry, Jesus," they said. How embarrassed they were! "We won't do it again."

Jesus just shook his head and went back to pray.

The disciples were determined to stay awake this time. They weren't letting Jesus down again. No way! But it was just so dark, and so quiet, and so peaceful, and . . . you guessed it. They fell asleep again.

(Have the children pull the strips on their sleepy faces to close the eyes.)

One more time, Jesus came back to his disciples and found them asleep.

"Wake up," Jesus told them.
(Have the children pull the strips on their sleepy faces to open the eyes.)

"There is no more time to sleep," Jesus said. "I've made my decision, and now it's time for me to go. I will do what God wants me to do."

Bring the puppet back out to talk to the children.

Have the puppet say: One, two, three times, Jesus asked the disciples to stay awake and pray for him. But one, two, three times, the disciples fell asleep. Have you ever wanted to do the right thing, but you didn't, because it was just too hard? I have. See, I want to go to my church's campout, but I'm afraid of the dark. I won't go outside at night, not even with my mom, not even with a great big flashlight. But I'm working on it. I know that God is with me all the time, especially when I'm having a bad time, so I'm talking to God about how to not be so afraid of the dark. You can do that too, you know, if there's something that's hard for you to do.

Have the puppet say goodbye until next week.

Bible Zone

Choose one or more activities to immerse your children in the Bible story.

Supplies:
Bible

Zillies®:
animal world beach ball

Bible Verse Toss-up

Before class blow up the **animal world beach ball**. Have the children stand in a circle.

Let a child hold the Bible open to Mark. Show the children where today's verse is found in the Bible. **Say the Bible verse for the children: "You want to do what is right, but you are weak"** (Mark 14:38). Have them repeat it several times until they are familiar with it.

Say: Just as we talked about earlier, all of us have things that are hard to do. Think of something that isn't easy for you. Maybe it's remembering to do a chore around the house. Maybe it's making new friends. Maybe it's math, or spelling, or science.

Tell the children you will toss the ball to one of them while you say the first word of the Bible verse. The children will continue tossing the ball and completing the Bible verse. The child who says the last word of the Bible verse should toss the ball to someone else. Encourage the person who catches the ball to say something that is hard for him or her to do. That person should sit down in the circle, and play will continue as before. Play until there is only one person standing.

Ask: Who is with us when we are struggling with something? *(God)*

Supplies:
none

Zillies®:
none

Which Is Harder?

Tell the children that you want them to think about things that are hard to do. You will give them two choices; they will tell you which one is harder.

Say: Which is harder, walking a mile or riding a mile? Which is harder, feeding a dog or feeding an alligator? Which is harder, eating lunch with a friend or eating lunch with a stranger who smells funny? Which is harder, spending money on something for yourself or spending money on something for a missionary in another country? Which is harder, studying for a science test or watching television? Which is harder, getting up early to help feed people who are homeless or sleeping late? Which is harder, smiling when we're mad or smiling when we're happy?

Ask: Who is with us when we are struggling with something hard? *(God)*

Life Zone

Choose one or more activities to bring the Bible to life.

Sing and Celebrate

Play the song "Love One Another" **(CD, Track 3)** through one time for the children. Play this simple tune again and encourage the children to sing along.

Love One Another

"Love one another,
love one another,
love one another,"
Jesus said.

"Love one another,
love one another,
love one another,"
Jesus said.

WORDS: John 15:17
MUSIC: George Donigian
Music copyright © 1991 Graded Press, admin. by The Copyright Co., Nashville, TN

Supplies:
CD player

Zillies®:
CD

Younger Elementary: Lesson 3

Life Zone

Choose one or more activities to bring the Bible to life.

Supplies:
Reproducible 3B
scissors
crayons or markers
glue
tape
yarn or ribbon
optional: instant-developing camera and film

Zillies®:
colored foam squares

Mosaic Wall Hanging

Give the children the wall hanging pages that you photocopied for the sleepy faces activity **(Reproducible 3B)**. Point out the phrase "God is with us" at the bottom of the wall hanging. Let the children draw a picture above the phrase to resemble themselves. *(If you have an instant-developing camera and film, take a photo of each child instead.)*

Set out the **colored foam squares** and glue. Encourage the children to make a colorful frame for their wall hanging by gluing the shapes around the edges in any design they choose. Tape a six-inch piece of yarn or ribbon to the top corners of each picture so that the children can hanging them on their wall at home.

Supplies:
CD player

Zillies®:
CD
bird warblers

Closing Time

Before class, experiment with a **bird warbler** to see how much water produces the best sound. Pour water into the bird warblers.

Play "Morning Has Broken" **(CD, Track 12)** to signal that it is closing time. By now the children should recognize the song and be able to sing along. Give bird warblers to half the children. Show the children how to blow through the warblers to make the birds sing. Play the song again. Let the children with bird warblers blow the warblers while the rest of the children sing along. Tell the children that others will get to blow the warblers next week.

Say the Bible verse for the students: "You want to do what is right, but you are weak" (Mark 14:38). Have the children repeat it.

Say: Remember, God is with you whenever things are hard to do. God will help you get through hard times. *(Have the children hold hands.)*

Pray: God, we know that Jesus' disciples wanted to stay awake that night in the garden, but they fell asleep anyway. We know that we don't always do what is right. Forgive us when we are weak and give us strength when we need it. Amen.

Have the children take home their sleepy faces and wall hangings. Collect the bird warblers. Wash them in soapy water before the next class.

Give each child a copy of the HomeZone to take home to parents.

Home Zone For Parents

Bible Verse
You want to do what is right, but you are weak.
                    Mark 14:38

Bible Story
    Matthew 26:36–46; Mark 14:32–42

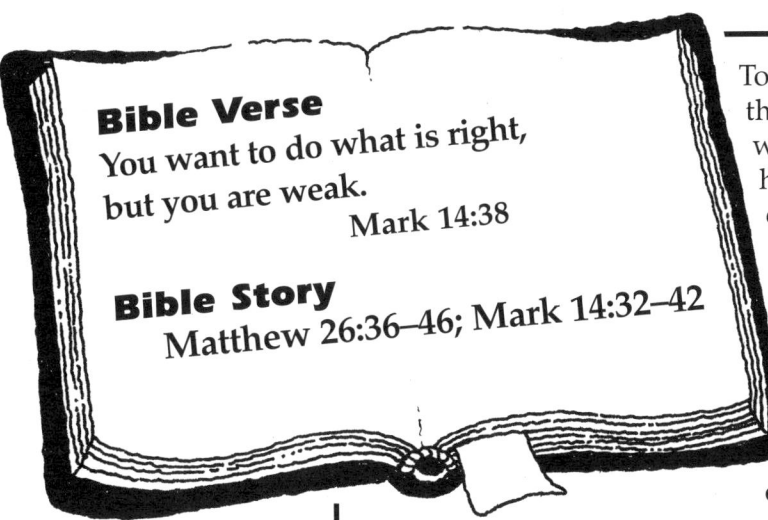

Today your child learned about Jesus' time in the garden of Gethsemane. The Last Supper was over and Jesus wanted to pray, so he took his disciples with him to the garden. The disciples that Jesus took with him fell asleep, even though Jesus asked them to keep him company. Remind your child that the disciples must have been ashamed when they realized that they had let Jesus down. Help your child understand that Jesus loved his disciples, even when they made mistakes, and that Jesus always loves your child, even when he or she makes a mistake.

Difficult Dance

In an open area of your home, have your child stand on one foot. Play music and encourage your child to dance while staying on one foot. See if your child can clap his or her hands at the same time. Join your child in the difficult dance. After the dance ends, remind your child that we sometimes have to do things that are hard. Talk about some of those things with your child. Remind your child that God is with us, even when we are struggling with something.

Easy Cheesy Puffs

You will need: cheddar cheese, all-purpose flour, salt, and pepper.

Preheat the oven to 375 degrees. Melt ½ cup cheddar cheese in the microwave oven. Let your child stir the cheese every 30 seconds until it is melted. Help your child measure and add in ¼ cup flour, ¼ teaspoon salt, and ¼ teaspoon pepper. Let your child use his or her hands to form the mixture into balls no more than an inch big. Place the balls on a greased baking sheet. Bake the cheesy puffs for 10 to 15 minutes, until they turn brown and puff up slightly.

God is with us when we have difficult things to do.

YOUNGER ELEMENTARY: LESSON 3   Permission granted to photocopy for local church use. © 2003 Abingdon Press.

Reproducible 3A

Permission granted to photocopy for local church use. © 2003 Abingdon Press.

BibleZone® LIVE

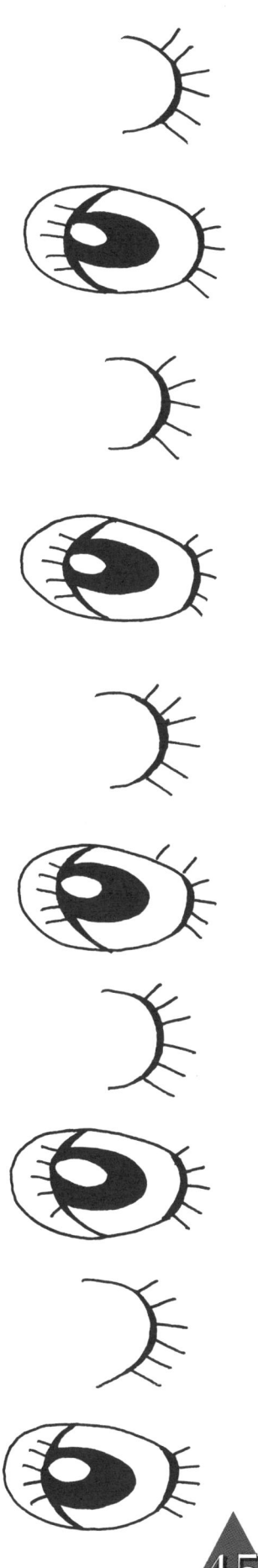

God is with us.

Younger Elementary: Lesson 3

Reproducible 3B

Permission granted to photocopy for local church use. © 2003 Abingdon Press.

45

4 BibleZone LIVE

I Don't Know Him!

Enter the Zone

Bible Verse
All who belong to the LORD, show how you love him.

Psalm 31:23

Bible Story
Luke 22:54-62; John 18:15-18, 25-27

Judas was not the only disciple who betrayed Jesus during his final days on earth; Peter also carries that dubious distinction, although Peter's betrayal was one of denial.

At the first Lord's Supper, Jesus told Peter that before the rooster crowed, Peter would deny three times that he knew Jesus. That would never happen, Peter said.

At that point, Peter's courage was strong. That courage was still intact a few hours later in the garden of Gethsemane. When the soldiers arrived to arrest Jesus, Peter drew his sword and cut off the right ear of the servant of the high priest. But at some point between Peter's brave act in the garden and Jesus' appearance before the high priest, Peter's courage deserted him. Three times he was identified as being a follower of Jesus. Each time, he forcefully and vehemently denied that he even knew Jesus.

As soon as the words "I don't know this Jesus!" left Peter's mouth the third time, the rooster crowed, and Jesus turned to look at Peter. How hard it must have been for Peter to return that look, knowing that he had betrayed Jesus. He may not have sold his Savior for a bag of gold, but he had turned his back on Jesus.

Where did Peter's courage go? It likely went to the same place that our own courage goes whenever we find ourselves in a difficult position and take the easy way out.

The children you teach will have had experience in choosing between right and wrong. Point out that not everyone makes the right decision all the time, not even Peter. Reassure your children that Jesus never stopped loving Peter, even though Peter made a bad choice, and that Jesus will never stop loving them.

BibleZone® LIVE

ZONE IN

We can stand up for Jesus.

Scope the Zone

ZONE	TIME	SUPPLIES	ZILLIES
Zoom Into the Zone			
Arrival Time	10 minutes	Reproducible 4A, CD player, pencils, nametags (page 170), tape or paper punch and yarn	CD
Rooster Tail Runaround	5 minutes	bandanna, scarf, or paper towel; tape	none
BibleZone			
One, Two, Three, Spin	5 minutes	Transparency 2, scissors, heavy paper or cardstock, paper punch, paper fasteners, (optional: overhead projector, posterboard, marker)	none
Rooster on a Stick	10 minutes	Reproducible 4B, paper punch, yarn, scissors, crayons or markers; tape, glue, or staples and staples; ruler, craft stick, or dowel rod	none
"I Don't Know This Man!"	10 minutes	roosters (optional: Bible-times headdress)	zoo animal finger puppet
Bible Verse Mixup	10 minutes	Bible, index cards, pen or marker, large envelopes	none
Say It With Signs	10 minutes	none	none
LifeZone			
Sing and Celebrate	5 minutes	CD player	CD
Stand Up for Jesus	5 minutes	none	none
Closing Time	5 minutes	CD player	CD, bird warblers

Zillies® are found in the **BibleZone® LIVE FUNspirational® Kit.**

YOUNGER ELEMENTARY: LESSON 4

Zoom Into the Zone

Choose one or more activities to catch your children's interest.

Supplies:
Reproducible 4A
CD player
pencils
nametags (page 170)
tape or paper punch and yarn

Zillies®:
CD

Arrival Time

Have the **CD** playing in the background. If possible, greet each child at the door as he or she arrives.

Say: Welcome to BibleZone Live, *(child's name)*! **I'm glad you're here.**

If the children do not know one another, have them continue to wear their nametags **(see page 170)**. Give the children the truth or lie sheet **(Reproducible 4A)**.

Say: Some of these statements are true. Some of them are lies. Circle the ones that are true. Draw an X through the ones that are lies.

Supplies:
bandanna, scarf, or paper towel
tape

Zillies®:
none

Rooster Tail Runaround

Have the children sit in a circle. Choose one child to be the rooster. Tape a bandanna, scarf, or paper towel to the small of that child's back.

Say: The rooster will walk around the outside of the circle, not touching anyone. But when the rooster taps someone on the head, that person should jump up and chase the rooster around the circle, trying to grab the rooster's tail.

The rooster wants to make it all the way around the circle and sit down in the open place without losing his or her tail. If the rooster makes it, the new child becomes the rooster. If not, choose a new rooster.

Play until every child has had a turn to be the rooster.

Say: In our Bible story today, we'll hear about a time when a rooster crowed.

We can stand up for Jesus.

48

BibleZone® LIVE

Bible Zone

Choose one or more activities to immerse your children in the Bible story.

One, Two, Three, Spin

Before class, photocopy onto heavy paper or cardstock and cut apart the spinner and the arrow **(Transparency 2)**. For an oversize spinner, use an overhead projector to project the image onto a piece of posterboard; trace the image. Cut out the spinner. Punch a hole in the center of the spinner and in the arrow, on the opposite end from the pointer. Use a paper fastener to loosely attach the arrow to the spinner.

Gather the children in a circle. Set the spinner in the center.

Say: In our Bible story today we'll hear about a time when a rooster crowed. But before that rooster crowed, something had to happen three times. Let's play a game where we have to think about things in threes.

Let each child take a turn spinning the arrow. When it stops spinning, encourage that child to think of three things that fit into whatever category the arrow is pointing to. If you have time, let the children make their own spinners to take home with them.

Supplies:
Transparency 2
scissors
heavy paper or cardstock
paper punch
paper fasteners
optional: overhead projector, posterboard, marker

Zillies®:
none

Rooster on a Stick

Before class photocopy and cut out the rooster **(Reproducible 4B)**. Leave the front and back connected along the top of the rooster. Fold along the top of the rooster so that the front and back are together. Use a paper punch to punch out the holes around the top and side edges. Cut four-feet pieces of yarn.

Give each child the two rooster sides. Let the children use crayons or markers to decorate the rooster.

Give each child a piece of yarn. Help the children thread the yarn through the bottom corner and tie it together to secure the yarn. Let the children thread the yarn through the holes, coming up through each hole, working around the rooster. Help the children tie off the yarn by tying it to the first knot.

Have each child create a handle for his or her rooster by taping, gluing, or stapling a ruler, craft stick, or dowel rod in the center at the bottom.

Supplies:
Reproducible 4B
paper punch
yarn
scissors
crayons or markers
tape, glue, or stapler and staples
ruler, craft stick, or dowel rod

Zillies®:
none

YOUNGER ELEMENTARY: LESSON 4

Bible Story

"I Don't Know This Man!"

By Betsi H. Smith

> This story is told by Peter. If you like, wear a Bible-times headdress to tell the story. (A piece of cloth draped over your head and tied with a rope or a thin scrap of cloth works well.) Or have someone else tell the story. Give that person a copy of the story ahead of time. See Lesson 1 (page 14) for suggestions on how to turn your storytelling area into a garden.
>
> Have the children bring their roosters to the storytelling area. Bring out the **zoo animal finger puppet**.

Have the puppet say: Remember me? You can call me (puppet's name). **It's storytime again. I hear that one of Jesus' disciples is telling our Bible story today. Here's how you can help: Listen for Peter to say, "I don't know this man." He'll say it three times. The first time, hold up your rooster and crow very softly. The next time Peter says, "I don't know this man," hold up your rooster again and crow a little louder. The last time Peter says, "I don't know this man," I want you to shake your roosters and crow as loudly as you can. Here we go.** (Set the puppet aside.)

(Peter starts to wander past the children. He stops. He speaks in a sad voice.)

I guess you've heard what I did last night. No? You haven't? Then I might as well tell you myself. You'll find out soon enough.

(Peter sits with the children.)

[It started last night. We were eating with Jesus, our teacher and friend, when out of nowhere, Jesus says that I'm going to tell people that I don't know him.

I couldn't believe Jesus would say that. I have been with him since the beginning. I'm proud to be a follower of Jesus. Honest.

"I would never do that!" I told him.

But Jesus said it was true.

"Before the rooster crows three times, you will say that you don't know me," Jesus said.

After we ate, we went with Jesus to the garden of Gethsemane. While we were there, some soldiers showed up and arrested Jesus. They took him away, like he was some kind of bad guy. Which he isn't. Sometimes Jesus says things that make people mad, but he does it because he loves people and wants them to love God.

I wanted to help Jesus, but what could I do? There were so many soldiers, and they were carrying swords. If they were out to get Jesus, would they be out to get Jesus' friends too? I thought they might.

The soldiers took Jesus to the high priest's house to see what the high priest would say about Jesus. I followed them. I was careful to blend in with the crowd. Some people who were there to watch the excitement built a fire while they waited to see what the high priest would say. It was a cold night, so we all huddled around the fire.

That's where it happened. A servant girl pointed at me and said, "That man right there was with Jesus."

I didn't think about what I was doing. I just opened my mouth and blurted, "Not me. I don't know this man." *(Have the children hold up their roosters and crow softly.)*

Then, just few minutes later someone else looked at me and said, "I recognize you. You're a friend of Jesus."

"No, I'm not," I insisted. "I don't know this man." *(Have the children hold up their roosters and crow a little louder.)*

And again, another person pointed at me and said, "That man is from the same place as Jesus. I know that he is with Jesus."

"Why won't you believe me?" I yelled. "You don't know what you're talking about! I don't know this man!"

(Have the children shake their roosters and crow as loudly as they can.)

Just after I said that, I heard a rooster crow. I looked over at Jesus, standing there surrounded by guards, and he looked at me sadly. I remembered Jesus telling me that I would say I didn't know him. I didn't believe him at the time, but that is exactly what I did.

I left that courtyard. I couldn't face Jesus anymore. I went off by myself, and I cried.

Bring the puppet back out to talk to the children.

Have the puppet say: Poor Peter. He had three chances to stand up for Jesus, and he didn't. Can you think of a time when you stood up for Jesus? I can. A friend of mine had a CD with some words on it that I knew were not good words to hear. I told my friend that I didn't want to listen to that CD. He could have gotten mad at me for saying that, but I knew that Jesus would not want me to listen to that CD.

Have the puppet say goodbye until next week.

YOUNGER ELEMENTARY: LESSON 4

Bible Zone

Choose one or more activities to immerse your children in the Bible story.

Supplies:
Bible
index cards
pen or marker
large envelopes

Zillies®:
none

Bible Verse Mix-up

Before class, create a set of Bible verse cards by writing the Bible verse on separate index cards, one word per card. You will need several sets of the cards. Put each set in a large envelope.

Have a student hold the Bible open to Psalms. Show the children where today's verse is found in the Bible. **Say the Bible verse for the students: "All who belong to the Lord, show how you love him"** (Psalm 31:23). Have them repeat it.

Divide the children into groups of three. Give each group an envelope containing the Bible verse cards.

Say: When I say go, open your envelopes and put the Bible verse in order. Then choose one person in the group to memorize the verse and come to me and say it.

Supplies:
none

Zillies®:
none

Say It With Signs

Teach the children how to say "I can stand up for Jesus" in American sign language.

Divide the children into pairs. Encourage the children to take turns saying the phrase to each other using sign language.

I: Fold all the fingers down with the exception of the pinky finger. Hold the hand close to the chest with pinky finger extended.
(can) stand: Form a "v" with the index and middle fingers. Then place the "v" on the left palm as though two fingers are walking.
up: Point up with the index finger.
for: With the index finger of the right hand, point to the forehead, circle down and point forward at eye level.
Jesus: Place the tip of the middle finger of the right hand into the left palm. Then place the tip of the middle finger of the left hand into the right palm.

Life Zone

Choose one or more activities to bring the Bible to life.

Sing and Celebrate

Play the song "Love One Another" **(CD, Track 3)** through one time for the children. Play this simple tune again and encourage the children to sing along.

Love One Another

"Love one another,
love one another,
love one another,"
Jesus said.

"Love one another,
love one another,
love one another,"
Jesus said.

WORDS: John 15:17
MUSIC: George Donigian
Music copyright © 1991 Graded Press, admin. by The Copyright Co., Nashville, TN

Supplies:
CD player

Zillies®:
CD

YOUNGER ELEMENTARY: LESSON 4

Life Zone

Choose one or more activities to bring the Bible to life.

Supplies:
none

Zillies®:
none

Stand Up for Jesus

Say: Today we've talked about Peter, who didn't stand up for Jesus even though he had three chances to do it. We can stand up for Jesus by standing up for what is right.

Have the children sit in chairs in a half-circle. Tell the children you are going to tell them about some problems. If they have a solution that shows a way to stand up for Jesus, they should stand up. Let the children who are standing tell their solutions. Remind the children that there may be more than one right answer to each problem.

Problem 1: A friend tries to talk you into stealing a candy bar from a store.
Problem 2: A person at school calls you a sissy because you have your Bible in your backpack.
Problem 3: A friend asks you to go to a baseball game, but it's on Sunday morning when you usually go to church.
Problem 4: At a sleepover, the other kids start telling dirty jokes.
Problem 5: Your parents don't want you to see PG movies without them, but the new movie that your friends are going to see is rated PG. The only way you can go is if you lie to your parents about which movie you're going to see.

Supplies:
CD player

Zillies®:
CD
bird warblers

Closing Time

Pour water into the **bird warblers**. Play "Morning Has Broken" **(CD, Track 12)** to signal that it is closing time. By now the children should recognize the song and be able to sing along. Give bird warblers to children who did not get to use them last week. Play the song again. Let the children with bird warblers blow the warblers while the rest of the children sing along.

Say the Bible verse for the students: "All who belong to the Lord, show how you love him" (Psalm 31:23). Have the children repeat it.

Help the children say, "I can stand up for Jesus" in sign language.

Pray: God, we love you, and we know how much you love us. We want to stand up for you. Give us the courage to tell the truth. Amen.

Have the children take home their spinners, if they made them, and roosters. Collect the bird warblers. Wash them in soapy water before the next class.

Give each child a copy of HomeZone to take home to parents.

Home Zone For Parents

Bible Verse
All who belong to the LORD, show how you love him.
Psalm 31:23

Bible Story
Luke 22:54–62; John 18:15-18, 25–27

Jesus had great faith in Peter, even saying that Peter would one day play a pivotal role in the formation of the new church. When Jesus told Peter that Peter would deny he knew Jesus three times before the night was over, Peter could not believe Jesus could think such a thing. But before dawn broke on the night of Jesus' arrest, Peter denied Jesus three times. Peter lacked the courage needed to stand up for Jesus, just as we sometimes lack courage to stand up for Jesus. Encourage your child to see that Jesus still loved and believed in Peter, just as Jesus loves us and believes in us, even though we sometimes make bad choices.

One, Two, Three, Toss

You will need: a deck of playing cards, three sheets of paper, and a marker.

Write the number *1* as large as possible on a plain sheet of paper. Do the same with the number *2* and the number *3*. Place the sheets of paper on the floor, with the number *3* the farthest away and the number *1* the closest. Let your child divide the deck of cards in half. Have your child keep half the cards. Take turns tossing a card at the numbers. Keep track of points. Remind your child that Peter said three times that he didn't know Jesus.

Quick and Tasty Pizzas

You will need: English muffins, pizza sauce or spaghetti sauce, shredded cheese, and your child's favorite pizza toppings.

Preheat the oven to 350 degrees. Separate the English muffins and lay them on a baking sheet. Help your child spoon spaghetti sauce or pizza sauce on each English muffin half. Let your child top the pizzas with his or her favorite ingredients and sprinkle on cheese. Bake until the cheese melts, about 10 minutes.

We can stand up for Jesus.

YOUNGER ELEMENTARY: LESSON 4   Permission granted to photocopy for local church use. © 2003 Abingdon Press.

Truth or Lie?

Circle the sentences that tell the truth. Draw an X through the sentences that tell a lie.

Grass is purple.

We walk on the ceiling.

Carrots are orange.

You wear shoes on your feet.

Giraffes can fly.

Apples grow on trees.

Cars run on root beer.

It snows during the winter.

Cows give milk.

Dogs have nine legs.

Clothes are made out of spinach.

One plus one is two.

Reproducible 4A

Younger Elementary: Lesson 4 **Reproducible 4B**
Permission granted to photocopy for local church use. © 2003 Abingdon Press.

5 BibleZone LIVE

The Garden Tomb

Enter the Zone

Bible Verse
God loved the people of this world so much that he gave his only Son.

John 3:16

Bible Story
Luke 23:44-56; John 19:38-42

As Jesus hung on the cross, the earth itself grieved. Although it was only three in the afternoon, the sun disappeared, and darkness covered the land.

Jesus' final words were a prayer: "Father, into your hands I commend my spirit" (Luke 23:46, NRSV). It's not surprising that Jesus prayed as his life came to an end. Jesus prayed about everything. Do you carry everything to God? Do you leave your worries on God's shoulders? Do you remember to thank God when things go well?

Because the sabbath was beginning, embalming Jesus' body had to wait. His followers barely had time to wrap his body in linen and lay it inside a tomb. The tomb belonged to Joseph of Arimathea, a follower of Jesus who approached Pilate and asked for permission to take away the body of Jesus. It is believed that the tomb was near Golgotha, the place of Jesus' crucifixion. This makes sense, since the lateness of the hour would have prevented Jesus' followers from taking the body any distance before the sabbath began.

The tomb would have been cut out of stone, perhaps four feet across and four feet high. When the stone was rolled against the doorway, the tomb would have been entirely black. How fitting that darkness could not contain the Light of the World! Three days later, Jesus left the darkness behind. During our darkest hours, we can find comfort in remembering that Jesus also spent time in darkness and despair. Just as he defeated the darkness, so can we.

This lesson may be difficult to teach since it begins with Jesus' death and ends with his body being placed in a tomb. Balance somber activities with upbeat activities. If some of your children seem disturbed by the story, remind them that Jesus' death is followed by Easter, when we celebrate that Jesus rose from the dead.

ZONE IN

Jesus is God's Son.

Scope the Zone

ZONE	TIME	SUPPLIES	ZILLIES®
Zoom Into the Zone			
Arrival Time	10 minutes	Reproducible 5A, CD player, pencils, nametags (page 170), tape or paper punch and yarn	CD
Time to Pay Up	5 minutes	page 171, scissors, small gift for each child	none
BibleZone®			
Show Me Your Face	5 minutes	none	none
How Did It Feel?	5 minutes	masking tape or chairs or classroom dividers (optional: sheet)	none
A Sad, Sad Day	10 minutes	Reproducible 5B, scissors	zoo animal finger puppet
Bible Verse Knockdown	10 minutes	Bible, mural paper or posterboard, pencil or chalk, two empty 2-liter bottles, wide-tip markers	vinyl animal print kick balls
Jesus Is God's Son	5 minutes	none	none
LifeZone			
Sing and Celebrate	5 minutes	CD player	CD
Stand-up Heart Card	10 minutes	paper, pencil, scissors, glue, colored tissue paper, crayons or markers	tracing rulers
Closing Time	5 minutes	CD player	CD, bird warblers

Zillies® are found in the **BibleZone® LIVE FUNspirational® Kit.**

YOUNGER ELEMENTARY: LESSON 5

Zoom Into the Zone

Choose one or more activities to catch your children's interest.

Supplies:
Reproducible 5A
CD player
pencils
nametags (page 170)
tape or paper punch and yarn

Zillies®:
CD

Arrival Time

Have the **CD** playing as the children enter the classroom. If possible, greet each child at the door as he or she arrives. Make eye contact with each child, getting down on the child's level, if possible.

Say: Welcome to BibleZone Live, (child's name)**! This is the place where we get to know the Bible, and we'll have fun doing it. I'm glad you're here today.**

If the children don't know one another, have them wear nametags **(see page 170)**.

Give the children the word search **(Reproducible 5A)**. Tell the children that the words they are searching for are the words in today's Bible verse: "God loved the people of this world so much that he gave his only Son" (John 3:16). Point out the verse printed at the bottom of the page. Encourage the children to find the words in the word search. Pair confident readers with children less confident about reading.

Supplies:
page 171
scissors
small gift for each child

Zillies®:
none

Time to Pay Up

Before class, photocopy the Gift Bill **(see page 171, top)**. You need one per child. Buy a small gift for each of the children. You might buy stickers, erasers, small boxes of crayons, or bookmarks. Have the gifts out of sight.

Say: I've got a gift for you. Would you like it now? (Expect the children to say yes.) **Okay. Here's the bill for your gift. If you'll pay me, I'll give you your gift.** (Hand out the bills. Expect the children to complain.) **What's wrong?** (Gifts are free; you shouldn't have to pay for gifts.) **You're right. Gifts are supposed to be free. Today we're talking about a gift that God gave us. God didn't want anything in return. God just loves us that much.**

Give the children the gifts you brought.

Zone IN®: Jesus is God's Son.

Bible Zone

Choose one or more activities to immerse your children in the Bible story.

Show Me Your Face

Gather the children in a half-circle.

Say: Did you know that you can tell people how you're feeling without ever saying a word? You can, you know. You can tell people how you're feeling by the expression on your face. *(Have a child come stand by you.)* **I'm going to whisper a feeling to** *(child's name)***, who will make a face that shows that feeling. I want all of you to guess what feeling** *(child's name)* **is showing you.**

After the children guess the first feeling, have another child take a turn. Play until every child has had a turn. Emotions can include happy, surprised, sleepy, sad, afraid, confused, mad, hungry, bored, and shy.

Supplies:
none

Zillies®:
none

How Did It Feel?

Before class, mark off a space that is about four feet long and about six feet wide. Use masking tape, classroom dividers, or chairs to mark off the space. If possible, locate it in a corner so that at least two of the four walls are solid. If you use chairs or room dividers, drape a sheet across them to make the space more closed in.

If possible, have all the children stand in the space.

Say: Today we're talking about a sad day. We're talking about the day that Jesus was killed. After Jesus died, some of his friends took his body to a tomb for burial. The tomb was like a small cave. It probably was about the size of the space in which we're standing.

Say: We practiced showing different feelings a few minutes ago. How do you think Jesus felt when he was hanging on the cross? How do you think Jesus' mother felt when she saw him? How do you think Jesus' friends felt when they put his body in the tomb? Our Bible story today tells us about the day when Jesus died. It's a sad story, but next week we'll hear the happy ending.

Supplies:
masking tape or chairs or classroom dividers
optional: sheet

Zillies®:
none

Zone In: **Jesus is God's Son.**

YOUNGER ELEMENTARY: LESSON 5

Bible Story

A Sad, Sad Day

By Betsi H. Smith

> Before class, photocopy and cut apart the questions that the children will ask during the Bible story (**Reproducible 5B**). This story is told by Joseph of Arimathea. Invite someone to visit your class to tell the story. Ask that person to wear a Bible-times headdress. Give that person a copy of the story ahead of time.
>
> Gather the children in the storytelling area. Give the six questions to six of your best readers. Point out the number on each question. Tell the children that you will call on them in order of the numbers. Bring out the **zoo animal finger puppet**.

Have the puppet say: Remember me? You can call me *(puppet's name)*. **Here I am again, so it must be time for our Bible story. Last time, one of Jesus' disciples told us about the night when Jesus was arrested. Today we have another friend of Jesus with us. He's going to tell us what happened to Jesus later that day. I know that some of you have questions for him. I'll just sit here and listen.** *(Set the puppet aside.)*

Hello. My name is Joseph of Arimathea. Can you say that? *(Have the children repeat the name.)* I was there the day that Jesus died on the cross. I want to tell you all about that day, but it's such a hard story. I don't know where to start. Maybe I could just answer your questions.

Have a child ask Question 1: Did you know Jesus?

Yes, I did. I believed that Jesus was a good person. Even more important, I believed that Jesus was the Son of God. And I wasn't alone. Every time that Jesus taught a crowd of people or healed someone who was sick, people started to believe that Jesus was God's Son.

Have a child ask Question 2: Why did the people want Jesus to die?

That's a good question. The religious leaders didn't want anyone to believe in Jesus. They wanted the people to listen to them and to follow all of their rules. Jesus told them that their rules were wrong. Jesus said that it was more important to love God and to love other people than it was to follow rules. The leaders hated Jesus for that, so they worked very hard to turn everyone against Jesus.

Have a child ask Question 3: Did anything strange happen just as Jesus died?

I'll say it did! Even though it was the middle of the day, all of a sudden, the

62

BibleZone® LIVE

sky turned as black as night. Inside our Temple, there's an area that's so special, no one is allowed to go inside it. When it got dark, the curtain that marked off that area ripped right in two, all by itself! Even one of the guards standing beside the cross when Jesus died said, "This man really was the Son of God."

Have a child ask Question 4: What happened to Jesus' body after he died?

I asked if I could take Jesus' body. I have a tomb in a garden close to where Jesus died. I wanted to do something special for Jesus, so I offered to bury him in my tomb. It wasn't a big tomb—just a hole in the side of a hill. I was told that I could have Jesus' body. So we very gently took his body down from the cross. I wanted to spend more time taking care of Jesus' body, but it was nearly the beginning of the sabbath, when Jews don't do any work. We just barely had time to wrap Jesus in cloth. Then we carried Jesus into the tomb and gently laid him down.

Have a child ask Question 5: Did the tomb stay open? Could anyone go in and out of it?

It didn't have a door. But what it did have was a big, heavy stone. It took several strong men to move that stone in front of the opening of the tomb. Once the stone was in place, no one could get in the tomb. Just to make sure, two guards were told to stand there and make sure that no one bothered Jesus' body.

Have a child ask Question 6: Is that the end of the story?

It's the end of the story right now. That all happened yesterday. Tomorrow morning, as soon as the Sabbath is over, some of the women who were friends of Jesus will go back to the tomb and will finish taking care of his body. (Pause) I'm going to miss Jesus. He spent his life telling everyone that God loves each one of us. God loves us so much that God sent Jesus to live on earth with us. God must really love us, to give up his only son like that.

Bring the puppet back out to talk to the children.

Have the puppet say: Today's story is a sad one, isn't it? It makes me sad to hear that Jesus died like that. But I'm happy to know that God loves us so much that God would send his only son to earth to be with us, even though God knew that Jesus would die one day. And best of all, I know a secret! Some of you might know the secret too. This isn't the end of Jesus' story. Next week we get to hear a great story.

Have the puppet say goodbye until next week.

Bible Zone

Choose one or more activities to immerse your children in the Bible story.

Supplies:
Bible
mural paper or posterboard
pencil or chalk
two empty 2-liter bottles
wide-tip markers

Zillies®:
vinyl animal print kick balls

Bible Verse Knockdown

Before class, write the Bible verse in large letters on two pieces of mural paper or posterboard for the two teams. Lightly write the verse with a pencil or with chalk. Post the pieces of paper or posterboard side by side.

Have a student hold the Bible open to John. Show the children where today's verse is in the Bible. **Say the verse for the students: "God loved the people of this world so much that he gave his only Son"** (John 3:16). Have them repeat it. Divide the children into two teams. Set two empty two-liter bottles on a table a few feet from the children. Give each team a **vinyl animal print kick ball**. Give one person from each team a wide-tip marker. Have those two people stand by the mural paper or posterboard. Have another person from each team stand by the bottles to retrieve the balls.

Say: When I tell you to start, one person from each team should toss the team's ball at a bottle. If that person misses, the next person in line takes a turn. When your team knocks over the bottle, you can trace over a word in the Bible verse. Your team wins when you have knocked over the bottle enough times to trace all the words in the Bible verse.

Supplies:
none

Zillies®:
none

Jesus Is God's Son

Tell the children you will say a poem. After you say each line, they should respond with "Jesus is God's son."

Leader: Jesus was born in Bethlehem.
Children: Jesus is God's son.
Leader: He loved his parents, and his parents loved him.
Children: Jesus is God's son.
Leader: Jesus told people, "God loves you."
Children: Jesus is God's son.
Leader: He never lied, so it must be true.
Children: Jesus is God's son.
Leader: "Just follow me," Jesus said.
Children: Jesus is God's son.
Leader: "I'll teach you how God wants you to live."
Children: Jesus is God's son.

Life Zone

Choose one or more activities to bring the Bible to life.

Sing and Celebrate

Play the song "Love One Another" **(CD, Track 3)** through one time for the children. Play this simple tune again, and encourage the children to sing along.

Love One Another

"Love one another,
love one another,
love one another,"
Jesus said.

"Love one another,
love one another,
love one another,"
Jesus said.

WORDS: John 15:17
MUSIC: George Donigian
Music copyright © 1991 Graded Press, admin. by The Copyright Co., Nashville, TN

Supplies:
CD player

Zillies®:
CD

Life Zone

Choose one or more activities to bring the Bible to life.

Supplies:
paper
pencil
scissors
glue
colored tissue paper
crayons or markers

Zillies®:
tracing rulers

Stand-up Heart Card

Before class, fold 8½- by 11-inch pieces of paper in half to make cards. On the front, sketch and then cut out a simple cross shape.

Gather the children in the art area. Give each child a card. Have the children open the cards and turn them face down. Have the children spread glue around the edge of the cross cutout and glue colored tissue paper over the cutout. Show the children how to hold the cross up to the light.

Say: God loved us so much that God gave Jesus to the world.

Let the children use a felt-tip marker to draw a heart around the cross cutout. Let them use the **tracing rulers** and markers or crayons to decorate the card. Encourage the children to write today's Bible verse on the inside of their card, showing them the verse written on the posterboard that was used in the "Bible Verse Knockdown" activity. Help any child who needs assistance. Show the children how to fold the card so it stands on its own.

Say: Take this card home to remind you how much God loves you.

Supplies:
CD player

Zillies®:
CD
bird warblers

Closing Time

Pour water into the **bird warblers**. Play "Morning Has Broken" **(CD, Track 12)** to signal that it is closing time. By now the children should be able to sing along. Ask the children to stand in a circle. Give bird warblers to children who did not get to use them last week. Play the song again. Let the children with bird warblers blow them while the rest of the children sing along.

Say the Bible verse for the students: "God loved the people of this world so much that he gave his only Son" (John 3:16). Have the children repeat it.

Say: It was a sad day when Jesus died. But next time we're going to talk about a happy day that followed that sad day.

Pray: God, thank you for giving us your son, Jesus. Help us remember how much you love us. Amen.

Have the children take home their stand-up heart cards and gifts. Collect the bird warblers and wash them in soapy water before next week.

Give each child a copy of the HomeZone to take home to parents.

Home Zone For Parents

Bible Verse
God loved the people of this world so much that he gave his only Son.
John 3:16

Bible Story
Luke 23:44–56; John 19:38–42

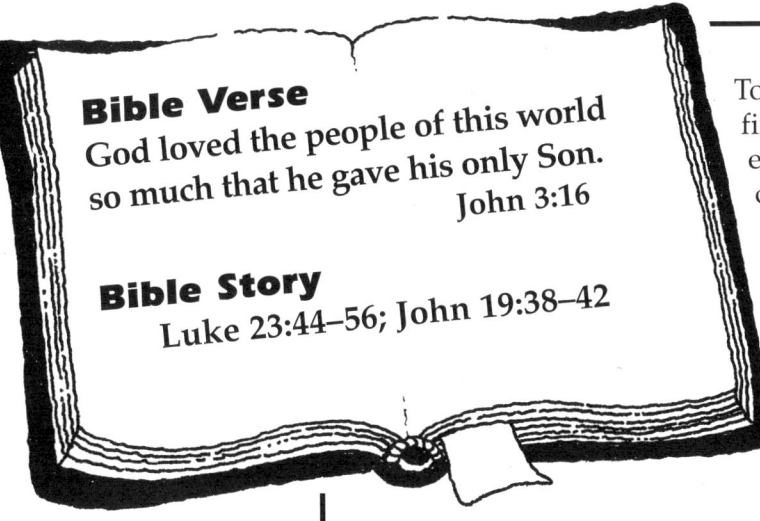

Today's lesson focused on Jesus' crucifixion. This was a time so dark that even the earth grieved, as darkness covered the land and the veil in the Holy Temple ripped in half. Talk with your child about Jesus' crucifixion, but downplay graphic details. Remind your child that God loves us so much that God gave us his son, Jesus. Point out that it's nearly Easter, when we celebrate because Jesus rose from the dead.

Easter Egg Cake

You will need: an unfrosted cake baked in an oval pan (or cut a round cake into an oval shape), canned vanilla frosting, food coloring

Make an Easter egg cake for your family to enjoy during the season. Place the cake on a large baking sheet. Mix a few drops of food coloring into one quarter cup frosting. (Repeat with several colors.) Set aside for now. Let your child help frost the cake with the white frosting. Decorate with the colored frosting. As you decorate, talk to your child about birds hatching from eggs. Because of this, eggs are used at Easter time to remind us of new life.

Opposites Attract

Help your child think of words that are opposite from each other. You say the first word and then encourage your child to come up with a word that is the opposite (*hot/cold, up/down, boy/girl, fast/slow, light/dark, happy/sad*). Remind your child that even though the day that Jesus died was sad, it was followed by a happy day.

Jesus is God's Son.

YOUNGER ELEMENTARY: LESSON 5 — Permission granted to photocopy for local church use. © 2003 Abingdon Press.

```
X R T S S O N A C E G
I K M O A Q H I S S U
W O R L D D W Y T B D
M F G P A J L T H A T
U S O E A M P R I T L
C V X O A H E A S C O
H E G P A O G A V E V
T H E L A N I K M P E
Q S U E A L W Y G O D
O F B D A Y F H J L N
```

God loved the people of this world so much that he gave his only Son.
(John 3;16)

Reproducible 5A

Permission granted to photocopy for local church use. © 2003 Abingdon Press.

Question 1: Did you know Jesus?

Question 2: Why did the people want Jesus to die?

Question 3: Did anything strange happen just as Jesus died?

Question 4: What happened to Jesus' body after he died?

Question 5: Did the tomb stay open? Could anyone go in and out of it?

Question 6: Is that the end of the story?

YOUNGER ELEMENTARY: LESSON 5

Reproducible 5B

Permission granted to photocopy for local church use. © 2003 Abingdon Press.

6 BibleZone LIVE

Good News

Enter the Zone

Bible Verse
Jesus isn't here! He has been raised from death.

Luke 24:6

Bible Story
Luke 24:1-12

Work was forbidden on the sabbath, and preparing a body for burial was considered work. Since the sabbath begins at sundown on Friday, Jesus' body had been placed in the tomb without the usual preparation for burial.

Jesus had cared for the needs, both physical and spiritual, of his followers for the past three years. Now it was their turn to take care of his needs, one final time. The women went to the tomb at dawn on Sunday to do what they did not have time to do on Friday. They were carrying spices that they were going to use to embalm Jesus' body. When the women arrived at the tomb, it was open, and Jesus' body was gone. Only the wrappings remained, much like only the cocoon remains when the butterfly breaks free and soars away.

The women were confused, until two men in brilliant clothes delivered the good news that dried the women's tears then and can dry our tears today. Jesus is alive! The tomb didn't hold him. Death lost, and we all won.

Avoid messy activities on Easter Sunday, since many of the children will be wearing new clothes. Comment on how nice they look, but balance your compliments on their clothing with other compliments: "Jason, I look forward to seeing your smile every week." "Whitney, I can always count on you to help me clean up our room."

As you help the children celebrate Easter, don't dwell too much on the details of Jesus' death. Answer questions honestly, but steer the conversation back to the resurrection. Yes, Jesus was crucified, but he rose again. Yes, Jesus was put into a tomb, but he didn't stay there. He lives in our hearts and in our lives. Now there's a reason to celebrate!

Zone In

God is more powerful than anything we can imagine, even death.

Scope the Zone

ZONE	TIME	SUPPLIES	ZILLIES®
Zoom Into the Zone			
Arrival Time	10 minutes	Reproducible 6A, CD player, pencils, crayons or markers (optional: page 170, tape or paper punch and yarn)	CD
Look Like Butterflies	10 minutes	Reproducible 6A, pencil, posterboard, scissors, yarn or ribbon, construction paper, crayons or markers, masking tape, stapler and staples, chenille stems	none
BibleZone®			
Becoming Butterflies	5 minutes	butterfly wings and antennae	none
Jesus Is Alive!	10 minutes	none	zoo animal finger puppet, kazoo
Signs of Easter	10 minutes	Reproducible 6B, crayons or markers	none
Bible Verse Egg Relay	5 minutes	Bible, plastic egg, serving spoon (optional: masking tape)	none
LifeZone			
Sing and Celebrate	5 minutes	CD player	CD
What's Most Powerful?	5 minutes	none	none
Closing Time	5 minutes	CD player	CD, bird warblers

Zillies® are found in the **BibleZone® LIVE FUNspirational® Kit.**

YOUNGER ELEMENTARY: LESSON 6

Zoom Into the Zone

Choose one or more activities to catch your children's interest.

Supplies:
Reproducible 6A
pencils
crayons or markers
CD player
optional: page 170,
    tape or paper
    punch and yarn

Zillies®:
CD

Arrival Time

Have the **CD** playing. Greet each child. If the children don't know one another, have them wear nametags **(see page 170)**. Give children the butterfly page **(Reproducible 6A)** you photocopied and cut apart before class. Have the children complete the butterflies' wings by copying the design on the left-hand wing onto the right-hand wing. Let the children use crayons or markers to decorate their butterfly wings.

Say: We talk about butterflies at Easter because butterflies remind us of new life. They start out as caterpillars, but after they spend some time in a cocoon, they become beautiful butterflies. Jesus died and spent three days in a tomb, but he rose again. That's why we celebrate Easter.

Supplies:
Reproducible 6A
posterboard
pencil
scissors
yarn or ribbon
construction paper
crayons or markers
masking tape
stapler and staples
chenille stems

Zillies®:
none

Look Like Butterflies

You will need one piece of posterboard for each child to make butterfly wings. Before class, cut posterboard in half, cutting across the long side. Draw a line down the center. Draw the outline of butterfly wings, filling the posterboard as completely as possible. Keep the outline simple. Cut out the wings. Using the first pair of wings as a pattern, cut out enough wings for each child to have a pair. Cut two pairs of wings from each sheet of posterboard.

Cut yarn or ribbon into 26-inch lengths; tie each piece into a loop. Tape two loops to the center of each pair of wings. The children will slip their arms through the loops and wear the wings like a backpack. Cut construction paper into one-inch strips that are long enough to circle a child's head. If necessary, tape two strips together.

Give each child a set of wings. Let the children use markers or crayons to decorate the wings. Point out the designs on the butterfly page **(Reproducible 6A)**, in case the children want to copy one of those designs. Show the children how to wear the wings. Adjust the loops as necessary. Help each child tape two chenille stems to the front of a construction paper strip, about two inches apart. Fit the strip to the child's head, taping the strip into a loop and cutting off any excess. Show the children how to curl the chenille stems at the end to make antennae.

Say: We talk about butterflies at Easter because butterflies remind us of new life. They start out as caterpillars, but after they spend some time in a cocoon, they become beautiful butterflies. Jesus died and spent three days in a tomb, but he rose again. That's why we celebrate Easter.

BibleZone® LIVE

Bible Zone

Choose one or more activities to immerse your children in the Bible story.

Becoming Butterflies

Have the children take off their wings and place them within reach. Let them continue to wear their antennae.

Say: Let's pretend that we are butterflies. How do butterflies start out? *(as caterpillars)* **Then what happens?** *(They spin a type of cocoon called a chrysalis.)* **Then what happens?** *(They turn into butterflies.)*

Encourage the children to do the actions as you say the poem below:

Crawl, little caterpillar, crawl on the ground.
No wings for you yet, just crawl 'round and 'round.
(Have the children hold their arms tight to their sides and wiggle their bodies.)

Spin, little caterpillar, spin your cocoon.
Make it nice and snug; it'll be your home soon.
(Have the children spin in a circle.)

Sleep, little caterpillar, sleep and grow.
When it's time to leave your cocoon, you'll know.
(Have the children close their eyes and rest their heads on their clasped hands.)

Push, little butterfly, push your way through.
No longer a caterpillar, your body's brand new.
(Have the children punch the air as if breaking out of a cocoon.)

Fly, little butterfly, fly here and there.
Your wings lift you up; you float on the air.
(Have the children put on their wings; let the children fly around the room.)

Say: We talk about butterflies at Easter because butterflies remind us of new life. We celebrate Easter because that's when Jesus rose from the dead.

Supplies:
butterfly wings and antennae

Zillies®:
none

YOUNGER ELEMENTARY: LESSON 6

Bible Zone Story

Jesus Is Alive!

by Betsi H. Smith

> Have the children sit in a circle. Give each child a **kazoo**. Show the children how to hum through the kazoos to make noise. Tell the children that there is a point in the story when they will get to play their kazoos as loudly as they can. Until then, they should place the **kazoos** on the floor in front of them. Bring out the **zoo animal finger puppet**.

Have the puppet say: It's me again, (puppet's name). I have been waiting all week to hear today's Bible story. Remember, I was a little sad when last week's story was over, because it was the story about Jesus dying on the cross. But I won't be sad this week.

(*Set the puppet aside for now. Teach the children the response and motions in the story below. Tell them that they can help you tell the Bible story by saying that response whenever you call on them. Let the children practice a couple of times.*)

Mary and her friends were sad. Can you show me a sad face? (*Let the children respond.*) They were sad because their friend Jesus was dead. They were going to the tomb where he was buried to take care of his body. They didn't know it, but they weren't going to be sad much longer!

Response:
Let's clap.
(Clap, clap)
Let's cheer.
(Say, "Hurray!")
We want the world to hear.
(Cup one hand behind ear; cup other hand behind other ear.)
Jesus is alive!
(Use sign language to say the words "Jesus" and "alive.")
Jesus is alive!
(Use sign language to say the words "Jesus" and "alive.")

Mary and her friends were surprised. Can you show me a surprised face? *(Let the children respond.)*

The big stone that was supposed to be in front of Jesus' tomb had been rolled out of the way. They ran to the tomb and looked in it. They looked for Jesus' body. But it wasn't there! The tomb was empty!

(Lead the children in the response and motions.)

Mary and her friends were scared. Can you show me a scared face? *(Let the children respond.)*

They were scared because, all of a sudden, two men were standing in front of them. It was hard to look at the men because their clothes were so bright. The women were so scared, they fell down on their faces. But the men had good news.

(Lead the children in the response and motions.)

Mary and her friends were happy. Can you show me a happy face? *(Let the children respond.)*

They were happy because the men told them that their friend Jesus wasn't dead after all. God was so powerful that God brought Jesus back from the dead.

(Lead the children in the response and motions.)

Mary and her friends were running. Can you run in place? *(Have the children stand and respond.)*

They were running because they wanted to tell the rest of Jesus' friends the good news.

(Lead the children in the response and motions.)

All of Jesus' friends were running and celebrating. Can you pick up your kazoos and then run in place while you play your kazoos? *(Let the children respond.)*

They were running and celebrating because they knew that Jesus was alive.

(Lead the children in the response and motions. Then have everyone sit down again.)

Bring the puppet back out to talk to the children.

Have the puppet say: I love that story! It doesn't matter how many times I hear it. I love it every time. That tomb was empty because God had brought Jesus back from the dead. Jesus is alive! How do you think Jesus' friends felt when they found out he was alive? *(Let the children respond.)* **How do you feel, knowing that Jesus is alive? It makes me happy. And I really want to hear your poem again. Could you do it for me one more time?** *(Lead the children in the response and motions.)* **Thanks!**

Have the puppet say goodbye until next week.

YOUNGER ELEMENTARY: LESSON 6

Bible Zone

Choose one or more activities to immerse your children in the Bible story.

Supplies:
Reproducible 6B
crayons or markers

Zillies®:
none

Signs of Easter

Give the children the Easter picture **(Reproducible 6B)** that you photocopied before class. Encourage the children to find the following signs of Easter: a cross, a butterfly, and an egg.

Say: These are all things that make us think of Easter. The cross reminds us that Jesus loved us so much that he died on a cross for us. The empty tomb reminds us that Jesus rose from the dead. The butterfly reminds us of new life. The egg reminds us of new life, too, because when the eggs crack open, baby birds are born.

Let the children decorate their Easter pictures.

Supplies:
Bible
plastic egg
serving spoon
optional: masking tape

Zillies®:
none

Bible Verse Egg Relay

Ahead of time, check to be sure that the plastic egg can be carried on the spoon.

Have a student hold the Bible open to Luke. Show the children where today's verse is in the Bible. **Say the Bible verse: "Jesus isn't here! He has been raised from death"** (Luke 24:6). Have the children repeat it.

Divide the children into two groups. Have the groups stand on opposite sides of the classroom. Show the children an egg. Remind the children that the egg is a symbol of Easter.

Give the first person in line in each group a spoon with the egg balanced in its bowl. That person will carry the egg in the spoon to the other side of the room. When that person reaches the other side, he or she will say the first half of the Bible verse *("Jesus isn't here!")* and give the spoon to the first person in line on that side. That person will carry the egg in its spoon to the first side. When he or she reaches the first group, that child should give the spoon and egg to the next person in line and say the second half of the Bible verse *("He has been raised from death.")*.

Continue until everyone has had a turn or until the children lose interest. To make the game more interesting, use chairs or masking tape to set up a winding obstacle course.

Life Zone

Choose one or more activities to bring the Bible to life.

Sing and Celebrate

Play the song "Mary Told the Good News" **(CD, Track 5)** for the children. Let them listen once all the way through. Play it again and encourage them to sing along on the refrain.

Mary Told the Good News

Refrain:
Mary told the good news,
 good news, good news!
Mary told the good news!
Jesus lives!

"Fear not," said the angel,
"And be not afraid.
For the one you seek is risen up
from the place where he was laid."

Refrain:
Mary told the good news,
good news, good news!
Mary told the good news!
Jesus lives!

What was that good news that
Mary heard the angel say,
While visiting the tomb that day
where the stone was rolled away?

Refrain:
Mary told the good news,
good news, good news!
Mary told the good news!
Jesus lives!

Go tell all the others
that death has lost its sting,
and Jesus goes before us now.
Alleluia! Let us sing!

Refrain:
Mary told the good news,
good news, good news!
Mary told the good news!
Jesus lives!

WORDS and MUSIC: John D. Horman; Copyright © 1993 Abingdon Press, admin. by The Copyright Co., Nashville, TN

Supplies:
CD player

Zillies®:
CD

YOUNGER ELEMENTARY: LESSON 6

Life Zone

Choose one or more activities to bring the Bible to life.

Supplies:
none

Zillies®:
none

What's Most Powerful?

Tell the children that you are going to name three things that are similar. Ask them to tell you which of the three in each group is the most powerful thing. Use the following examples: plastic knife/pocketknife/chainsaw; tricycle/bulldozer/motorcycle; twig/tree trunk/blade of grass; water hose/squirt gun/fire hose; fan/tornado/breeze; ant/kitten/elephant; (Make this the last example) people/animals/God.

Say: God is more powerful than anything else. God is even more powerful than death. Jesus rose from the dead because God is so powerful.

Supplies:
CD player

Zillies®:
CD
bird warblers

Closing Time

Play "Morning Has Broken" **(CD, Track 12)** to signal that it is closing time. Let the children sing along. Give **bird warblers** to children who did not get to use them last week. Play the song again. Let the children with bird warblers blow the warblers while the rest of the children sing along.

Say the Bible verse for the students: "Jesus isn't here! He has been raised from death" (Luke 24:6). Have the children repeat it. Have the children say, "Jesus is alive" in American Sign Language.

Have the children stand in a circle.

Pray: God, we know that your son, Jesus, rose from the dead on Easter Sunday. On this Easter Sunday we want to thank you for loving us so much that you sent us your Son. Help us to love other people the way that you love us. Amen.

Have the children take home their butterfly wings, antennae, and Easter picture. Collect the bird warblers. Wash them in soapy water before you use them again.

Give each child a copy of the HomeZone to take home to parents.

BibleZone® LIVE

Home Zone For Parents

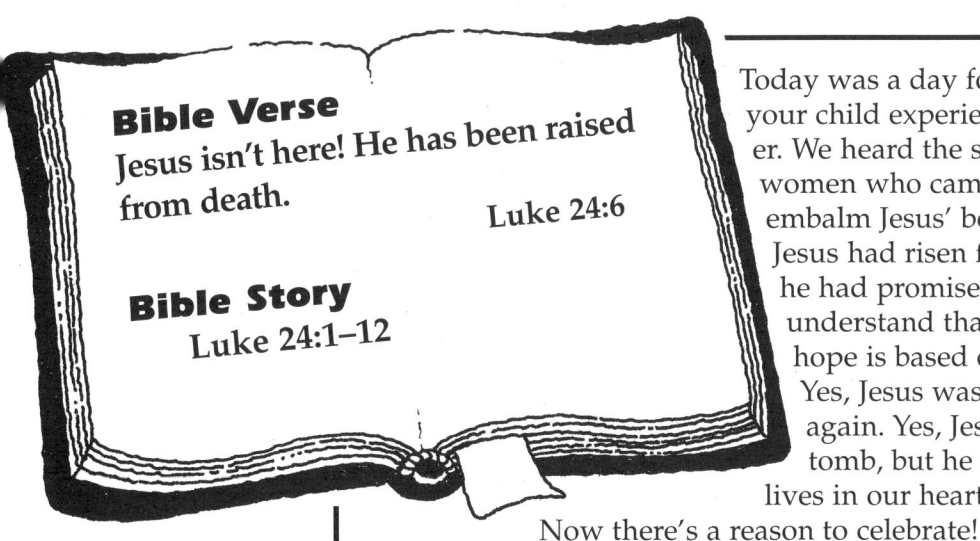

Bible Verse
Jesus isn't here! He has been raised from death. Luke 24:6

Bible Story
Luke 24:1–12

Today was a day for celebration, as your child experienced the joy of Easter. We heard the story about the women who came to the tomb to embalm Jesus' body, only to find that Jesus had risen from the dead just as he had promised. Help your child understand that, as Christians, our hope is based on Jesus' resurrection. Yes, Jesus was crucified, but he rose again. Yes, Jesus was put into a tomb, but he didn't stay there. He lives in our hearts and in our lives. Now there's a reason to celebrate!

Paint a Rock

Choose a flat rock. Have several colors of paint on hand. Encourage your child to paint a symbol of Easter on the rock. Let your child choose which symbol he or she wants to paint. Suggest a cross, a tomb, a butterfly, or an egg. Let the paint dry.

Sandwich Puzzle

You will need: your child's favorite sandwich.

The next time you are fixing your child a sandwich, instead of simply cutting it in half, do something different. Use a small knife to cut the sandwich into nine puzzle pieces. Mix the pieces up on a paper plate. Let your child solve the puzzle and then eat it!

Zone In: God is more powerful than anything we can imagine, even death.

Younger Elementary: Lesson 6 — Permission granted to photocopy for local church use. © 2003 Abingdon Press.

Reproducible 6A

Permission granted to photocopy for local church use. © 2003 Abingdon Press.

BibleZone® LIVE

Younger Elementary: Lesson 6 — **Reproducible 6B**

Permission granted to photocopy for local church use. © 2003 Abingdon Press.

BibleZone LIVE

No Garden at All

Enter the Zone

Bible Verse
As soon as God spoke the world was created; at his command, the earth was formed.

Psalm 33:9

Bible Story
Genesis 1:1-13

The word *Genesis* means "beginning" in Greek, and that's what the Book of Genesis is, an account of the beginning of the world. Step by step, breaking the process down into days, Genesis outlines how the earth went from "a formless void" into a self-sustaining, thriving planet, full of life.

This week's Scripture describes the first three days of Creation. On the first day, God created night and day. On the second day, God created sky and water. On the third day, God created land and vegetation.

Each day, God looked over what had been created that day and pronounced the creations good. And indeed, they were good. Night and day give us structure. Land gives us a firm foundation beneath our feet. Water is necessary to sustain all life. Vegetation gives shade above us, a soft surface below us, and nourishment for all kinds of living things.

Your class will be learning about Creation over the next few weeks. During this time, look for ways for the children to experience nature in a hands-on manner. If possible, take them on walks out of doors to look for signs of Creation—trees, flowers, leaves, a bird or a lizard, a butterfly or an ant. If it isn't possible to go outside, bring nature in. Even a glass of water can be an example of Creation.

As the children you teach learn about the Great Creator, give them plenty of opportunities to be creators themselves. Give them craft activities with few restrictions so that they can let their own creativity be their guide. Let them draw, paint, build, glue, and sculpt. Praise their efforts. Remember that for children, the process of creation is just as important as the completed product.

ZONE IN

God created everything that is.

Scope the Zone

ZONE	TIME	SUPPLIES	ZILLIES®
Zoom Into the Zone			
Arrival Time	10 minutes	Reproducible 7A, CD player, pencils	CD
Earth, Water, Sky	5 minutes	none	none
BibleZone®			
Touch the Earth	10 minutes	empty egg carton, potting soil, pie tin, seeds, plastic spoons, paper, scissors, pen, tape, toothpicks	none
Touch the Water	10 minutes	dishpan, water, small measuring cup or spoon, planted seeds, coins, objects to drop into water, hand towels	magnifying glasses
See the Sky	5 minutes	construction paper or heavy paper, scissors, ruler, drinking straws, tape	none
In the Beginning	10 minutes	none	zoo animal finger puppet
Creation Picture	10 minutes	see page 88	none
LifeZone			
Sing and Celebrate	5 minutes	CD player	CD
Bible Verse Pass	5 minutes	Bible	animal world beach ball
Closing Time	5 minutes	Transparency 1, overhead projector, CD player	CD

Zillies® are found in the **BibleZone® LIVE FUNspirational® Kit.**

YOUNGER ELEMENTARY: LESSON 7

Zoom Into the Zone

Choose one or more activities to catch your children's interest.

Supplies:
Reproducible 7A
CD player
pencils

Zillies®:
CD

Arrival Time

Have the **CD** playing as the children enter the classroom. Greet each child at the door as he or she arrives.

Say: Welcome to BibleZone Live, (child's name)**! I'm glad you're here.**

Give the children the "Where's My Kite?" page **(Reproducible 7A)** that you photocopied before class. Encourage the children to identify who is flying each kite by tracing the kite strings back to the children who are holding them. [Answer: 5, 4, 3, 1, 2]

Say: Kites fly in the sky. We're talking about the sky in today's lesson.

Teacher Tip: If your church is in a location where you can take the children outside, plan to spend some of your class time out of doors as you study Creation. Arrange for extra adult supervision, if necessary.

Supplies:
none

Zillies®:
none

Earth, Water, Sky

When all the children have arrived, play a listening game. Gather the children in an open area. Have them stand facing you.

Say: Today we're talking about the earth and how it began. Before God created people or animals, God created places for them to live. God created land, water, and sky. Let's use these words to play a listening game.

Tell the children that you are going to call out either "land," "water," or "sky." If you call out "land," they should bend over and touch the floor. If you call out "water," they should pretend to swim. If you call out "sky," they should jump up as high as they can.

Say: If I call out "God created the world," I want you to stretch out your arms and spin in a circle.

Play as long as the children show interest. If you have time, let volunteers take turns calling out commands.

BibleZone® LIVE

Bible Zone

Choose one or more activities to immerse your children in the Bible story.

Touch the Earth

Pour potting soil into a pie tin. Let each child touch the soil. Help the children as they plant seeds. Let each child use a plastic spoon to spoon a small amount of potting soil into an egg-carton cup. Put in enough soil to fill the cup about half full. Show the children how to sprinkle seeds into the cups and spoon more soil on top. (If necessary, call your local garden center to find out which plants grow rapidly in your region.) Write the children's names on small slips of paper. Tape the paper to toothpicks. Stick the toothpicks into the soil in each cup to identify each child's planting. Tell the children they can check their seeds over the next few weeks to see what happens.

Supplies:
empty egg carton
potting soil
pie tin
seeds
plastic spoons
paper
scissors
pen
tape
toothpicks

Zillies®:
none

Touch the Water

Set a dishpan full of water in the center of a table. Let each child run his or her fingers through the water. Have a small measuring cup or spoon on hand. Let the children use the cup to pour a small amount of water over the seeds they just planted. Let the children drop various items into the dishpan of water to see what will happen to them. Which ones float? Which ones sink? Drop several coins into the water. Ask the children if the coins look different under the water. Let the children use the **magnifying glasses** to look at objects that you drop under the water. Have towels on hand for the children to dry their hands.

Supplies:
dishpan
water
small measuring cup
  or spoon
planted seeds
coins
objects to drop into
  water
hand towels

Zillies®:
magnifying glasses

See the Sky

Let the children make sky surfers. Before class, cut construction paper or another heavy paper into strips one inch wide. Make half of the strips nine inches long and the other half seven inches long. Give each child a drinking straw and two paper strips. Have the children fold each strip into a loop and tape each loop shut. Help them tape one loop about an inch in from one end of the straw and the other loop about an inch in from the other end. Show the children how to hold the straw between the loops and sail it gently through the air. Let them see how far they can throw their sky surfers. If possible, take the children outside. Encourage them to look closely at the sky. Is it cloudy or clear? Let them sail their sky surfers.

Supplies:
construction paper or
  heavy paper
scissors
ruler
drinking straws
tape

Zillies®:
none

YOUNGER ELEMENTARY: LESSON 7

Bible Zone Story

In the Beginning

by Betsi H. Smith

> **Say: Before God created people, or animals, or even plants, God created places for them to live. God created the earth, the water, and the sky.**
>
> Have the children sit in the storytelling area. Bring out the **zoo animal finger puppet**.

Have the puppet say: Hello, everyone! Remember me, *(puppet's name)*? Have you ever looked up at the sky and said, "God made that"? Have you ever picked a flower and said, "God made that"? Today and the next few weeks, we're going to talk about the beginning of the world, when God made the sky and God made flowers and God made—well, God made everything there is, even me and even you. So let's get started, okay?

Leah lifted her hand to her mouth to cover a yawn. She was sleepy, but she wasn't ready to go inside yet. She stretched out on the ground and scooted down until her head was resting on a smooth stone. She looked over at the house. Her mother had lit the oil lamps and had unrolled the woven mats upon which the family slept.

Leah smiled as she looked up at the night sky. The breeze tickled her nose.

"Are you saying 'Thank you'?" Poppa asked. Leah had not heard him come outside.

"Thank you for what?" Leah was confused. She had already thanked her mother for supper. That was hours ago.

"Thank you to God," Poppa said. "The way you were looking up at the sky, I thought maybe you were thanking God for it."

Leah giggled. "Oh, Poppa, you don't say thank you for the sky," she said. "The sky is just the sky. It's always been there."

"Not always," he said. "Not in the beginning."

"The beginning of what?" Leah asked.

"Why, the beginning of everything, Leah," Poppa said. "The beginning of the world. The Bible tells us about how it happened."

"Tell me," Leah said. "Please, Poppa?"

Poppa bent his long legs and sat down beside her on the hard dirt ground.

"In the beginning," Poppa began, "there was nothing. No shape. No color. No life. No world. Nothing but darkness." Leah's eyes were round. "What happened?"

BibleZone® LIVE

"First, God said, 'Let there be light,'" Poppa said. "And there was light, just like that. So the world had light in the day and dark at night. We use the light to help us see what we're doing during the day."

"And we can use the dark to help us sleep at night," Leah added.

"That's right," Poppa said. "After God created day and night, God created the sky. During the day, if we don't see any clouds in the sky, we know that it's probably going to be sunny. And if the sky turns dark, then —"

"Then it's about to rain!" Leah said. "What did God create after the sky?"

"Until then, the world was covered with water," Poppa said. "God caused dry ground to rise up out of the water. God called the dry land earth, and God called the water seas."

Leah ran her hand along the ground beside her and lifted it to show Poppa the dirt that was clinging to it.

"Was this part of the earth that God created?" she asked.

"It was, and so is sand and red clay and even that rock that your head is resting on," Poppa said. "All the dry land was created by God, and so was all the water. That means the ocean that we can see in the distance during the day. It also means the small creek that runs behind our house, where you get our water every day."

"Did God create people next?" Leah asked.

"No, not yet," Poppa said. "God wanted everything to be just right before he created people. God knew they would need food to eat and something over their heads to give them shelter, so God created plants and trees and flowers."

"Like the palm tree growing beside the house," Leah said.

"Like the palm tree, and like the wheat that you help your mother cut," Poppa said. "And like the fig tree that gives us fruit. God created all of that, and much more. That's why, when I saw you looking up, I thought you were thanking God for the sky and the earth and everything on it."

"I'm going to, when I go to bed tonight and say my prayers," Leah said. She had a lot to think about. God had created everything, even the sky!

Bring the puppet back out to talk to the children.

Have the puppet ask: Do you remember what God created first? *(day and night)* **And what came next?** *(sky)* **And then?** *(earth and water)* **And then?** *(plants, trees, flowers)* **I wonder when God created animals. I hope we talk about that soon.**

Have the puppet say goodbye until next week.

YOUNGER ELEMENTARY: LESSON 7

Bible Zone

Choose one or more activities to immerse your children in the Bible story.

Supplies:
Reproducible 7B
paper
green and blue crayons, markers, or paint
glue
paintbrushes
scissors
white paint
cotton balls
optional: page 169

Zillies®:
none

Creation Picture

Give each child a sheet of white paper (11 by 17 inches, if you have it). Make sure each child's name is on his or her paper. Tell the children that over the next few weeks, they are going to make their own Creation pictures, just as God created the world.

Say: First God created day and night, water and sky, and land and plants. We know that God created night too, but we're going to create a daytime picture.

Encourage the children to create land by using crayons, markers, or paint to color the bottom half of their papers green. Encourage the children to create sky by using crayons, markers, or paint to color the top half of their papers blue. (Watercolor paint gives a soft effect, if you choose to use it.)

Point out the body of water on the garden page (**Reproducible 7B**) that you photocopied before class. Show the children how to use a blue felt-tip marker or crayon to draw horizontal scalloped lines across the water to resemble waves. Have the children cut out and glue their bodies of water somewhere on the bottom half of their pictures. Add a few drops of blue paint to clear glue. Let the children paint the mixture across their water. When it dries, it will be shiny.

Pour white paint onto a paper plate. Have the children make clouds in the sky on their pictures by dabbing cotton balls into white paint and then dabbing them onto the top half of their pictures. Or let the children glue cotton balls to their pictures.

Have the children color and cut out the trees, plants, and flowers (**Reproducible 7B**) and glue them somewhere on the bottom half of their pictures.

Set the pictures aside. Assure the children that they will take their Creation pictures home with them when the pictures are finished in a few weeks.

Teacher Tip: If you choose, let the children make shoebox gardens instead of flat pictures. Suggestions are on page 169.

God created everything that is.

Life Zone

Choose one or more activities to bring the Bible to life.

Sing and Celebrate

Play the song "Everybody Give Thanks!" **(CD, Track 11)**. Let the children have fun moving to the music and singing along.

Everybody Give Thanks!

God made the bugs and birds and bees.
God made turtles, toads, and trees.
God made everything we see.
God did this all for you and me!

Refrain:
Everybody give thanks!
Everybody give thanks!
Everybody give thanks to God above
for showering us with his love.
Everybody give thanks!
Everybody give thanks!
Everybody give thanks for all those blessings from above!

God made the ground beneath our feet.
God made all the food we eat.
God made the people that we meet.
God did this all for you and me!

Refrain

We thank God every day for all God sends our way.
And every time we pray, we say, "We thank you, God!"

Refrain

WORDS and MUSIC: Dan McGowan
Copyright © 1994 Dan McGowan. Used by permission.

Supplies:
CD player

Zillies®:
CD

God created everything that is.

Life Zone

Choose one or more activities to bring the Bible to life.

Supplies:
Bible

Zillies®:
animal world beach ball

Bible Verse Pass

Blow up the **animal world beach ball.** Have a student hold the Bible. Show the children where today's verse is found in the Bible. **Say the Bible verse for the students: "As soon as God spoke the world was created; at his command, the earth was formed"** (Psalm 33:9). Have them repeat it, breaking it down into four phrases to make it easier to remember (As soon as God spoke/the world was created;/at his command,/the earth was formed.)

Have the children stand in a circle, then turn to the left so that the each child is facing the back of the child in front of him or her. Join the circle yourself, holding the animal world beach ball.

Say: I'll start by passing the ball behind me over my head and saying the first word of the Bible verse. When the ball reaches you, pass it behind you over your head and say the next word of the Bible verse.

Once the children are comfortable saying the Bible verse, vary the activity by passing the ball between the knees; then alternate over the head and between the knees.

Supplies:
Transparency 1
overhead projector
CD player

Zillies®:
CD

Closing Time

Play "Awesome God" **(CD, Track 8)** to signal the children that it is closing time. Review the American Sign Language for the song **(Transparency 1).** Play the song again. Encourage the children to sign and sing along.

Have the children stand in a circle.

Say the Bible verse for the students: "As soon as God spoke the world was created; at his command, the earth was formed" (Psalm 33:9). Have the children repeat it.

Pray: God, you are the Great Creator. Before anything else existed, you were there. Thank you for loving us enough to give us a beautiful world. Help us to remember to say thank you for the beauty that is all around us. Amen.

Have the children take home their sky surfers.

Give each child a copy of the HomeZone to take home to parents.

Home Zone For Parents

Bible Verse
As soon as God spoke the world was created; at his command, the earth was formed.
Psalm 33:9

Bible Story
Genesis 1:1–13

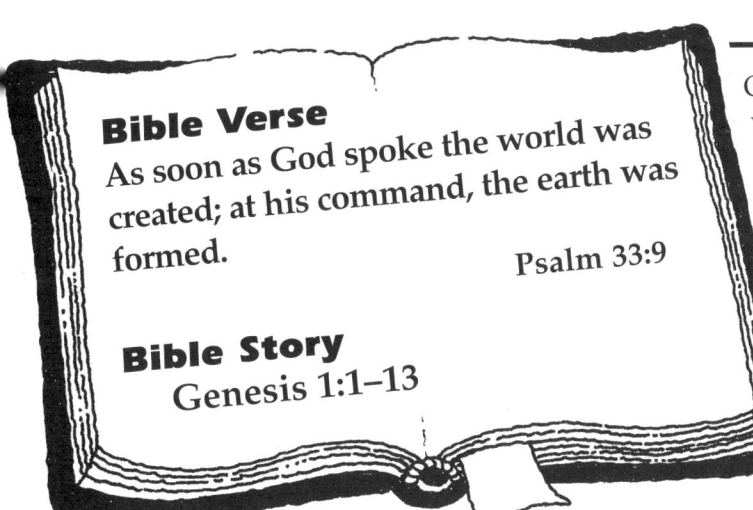

Over the next few weeks, your child will be studying Creation. Today your child learned about the beginning of Creation, when God created night and day; sky and water; and earth and plants. Take advantage of this time to help your child develop an appreciation for the earth and everything on it. Go on a nature walk with your child. Notice the changing seasons. Give your child responsibility for taking care of a plant or an animal. Don't forget to say thank you prayers for God's creation.

What Do You See?

Spread a blanket or bath towel out on the ground. Lie on the blanket or towel beside your child. Study the clouds. Encourage your child to look for shapes in the clouds. Can your child see animal shapes? What about faces? Can your child see any clouds that are shaped like letters or numbers? Point out how the clouds move across the horizon.

Great Big Earth Cookie

You will need: break-away sugar cookie dough or tube-shaped sugar cookie dough, canned vanilla frosting, blue and green food coloring.

Cut the tube-shaped cookie dough into slices. Place the dough in a 9-inch round cake pan. Or place the entire block of break-away dough into the pan. (Break-away cookie dough is in the refrigerated section of the grocery store.) Let the dough soften. Grease your child's hands with cooking oil spray or butter. Let your child spread the dough out to fill the pan. Bake according to the directions on the package. (Because of the thickness, you may have to bake this giant cookie longer than the directions indicate. Remove the cookie when the edges start to brown and the center is firm. When the cookie has cooled, mix a few drops of blue food coloring with frosting in a small bowl. Let your child use a plastic knife to frost the entire surface of the cookie. In a second bowl, mix a smaller amount of frosting with green food coloring. Have your child randomly place green frosting in several spots on the cookie. If you have a globe, show your child that his or her giant cookie resembles the earth.

God created everything that is.

Reproducible 7A

Younger Elementary: Lesson 7

Reproducible 7B

Permission granted to photocopy for local church use. © 2003 Abingdon Press.

93

8 BibleZone LIVE

Let There Be Light

Enter the Zone

Bible Verse
I often think of the heavens your hands have made, and of the moon and stars you put in place.
Psalm 8:3

Bible Story
Genesis 1:14-19

On the fourth day of Creation, God made the sun, the moon, and the stars. God set up our world so that our very lives depend on the sun. The sun provides heat to keep our environment inhabitable. It makes photosynthesis possible so that plants can grow and provide us all with nourishment. It's rising and setting signal daytime and nighttime, letting us know when it is time to be active and when it is time to rest.

The moon illuminates our nights and controls the oceans' tides. The moon helps us mark the passing of time as it goes from being fully visible to barely visible and fully visible again over a month's time.

The stars provide endless fascination for astronomers, who track their movements and changes. In past days, sailors depended on the stars as navigational guides, which allowed the sailors to navigate wide, treacherous bodies of water.

In the beginning, God gave light to the world through the sun. Many centuries later, God again gave light to the world, a light that can never be hidden by clouds or dimmed by darkness. God gave us God's son, Jesus, the true Light of the World.

God has indeed created a beautiful world. Even though we know this, it's easy to get caught up in everyday activities and to forget to stop and take a look around us.

Encourage the children you teach to pay attention to their world: the colors of a rainbow, the shapes of a cloud, and the texture of a tree. If you can help the children learn to find joy in the beauty that is all around them, you will be giving them a priceless gift that will serve them well throughout their lives.

God made the sun, the moon, the stars, and the planets.

Scope the Zone

ZONE	TIME	SUPPLIES	ZILLIES®
Zoom Into the Zone			
Arrival Time	10 minutes	Reproducible 8A, CD player, pencils	CD
Star Search	5 minutes	Reproducible 8B (top), scissors, watch or timer	baskets
BibleZone®			
Shine-Through Stars	15 minutes	Reproducible 8B (top); small paper cups, thick hand towels or dish towels, push pins or sharpened pencils	mini flashlight keychains, baskets
Squares and Stars	5 minutes	page 172, markers (optional: chalkboard and chalk, or dry erase board and markers)	none
Sun, Moon, Stars, Planets	10 minutes	none	zoo animal finger puppet
Punch and Play	5 minutes	Bible; Reproducible 8B; paper, plastic, or foam cups; paper napkins; tape or rubber bands	none
Add to Creation	5 minutes	see page 100	none
LifeZone			
Sing and Celebrate	5 minutes	CD player	CD
Bible Verse Bracelet	10 minutes	see page 102	tracing rulers
Closing Time	5 minutes	Transparency 1, overhead projector, CD player	CD

Zillies® are found in the **BibleZone® LIVE FUNspirational® Kit.**

YOUNGER ELEMENTARY: LESSON 8

Zoom Into the Zone

Choose one or more activities to catch your children's interest.

Supplies:
Reproducible 8A
CD player
pencils

Zillies®:
CD

Arrival Time

Have the **CD** playing as the children enter the classroom. Greet each child at the door as he or she arrives.

Say: Welcome, *(child's name)*! **I'm glad you're here today.**

Give each child the space picture (**Reproducible 8A**) that you photocopied before class. Have the children cross out five things that don't belong in the picture. Have them circle the words hidden in the picture: *star, sun, moon,* and *planets.*

Say: Last week we started talking about God creating the world. This week we're talking about when God created the sun, moon, stars, and planets.

Supplies:
Reproducible 8B (top)
scissors
watch or timer

Zillies®:
baskets

Star Search

Before class, make two photocopies of **Reproducible 8B.** You will use the top of the page (the stars, moons, plants, and suns) for this activity. Cut the items apart. It will be easier to cut irregular shapes around each item, instead of cutting each item out on the lines. Hide the items around the room and set the baskets on a table.

Make enough additional copies of the bottom of the page so that you have one for each child. Set these papers (Bible verse stars) aside until later in the lesson. When all the children have arrived, gather them together. Divide them into two teams. Show them the baskets that you have set out on a table. Have each team choose one person to stand by his or her team's basket.

Say: There are stars, suns, moons, and planets hidden throughout the room. When I say "Go," see how many of them you can find in two minutes. When you find one, bring it to your team member, who will put it in your team's basket.

After the two minutes are up, count the stars, moons, suns, and planets in each basket. Stars are worth one point; moons are worth three points; planets are worth four points; and suns are worth five.

Say: Today we're talking about when God created the sun, moon, stars, and planets.

96

BibleZone® LIVE

Bible Zone

Choose one or more activities to immerse your children in the Bible story.

Shine-Through Stars

Recruit additional people (enough so that children can work in groups of two or three, each with an adult) to help with this activity. If this is not possible, have some of the children work on the next activity (Squares and Stars) while you supervise others making their Shine-Through Stars. Keep rotating children until all have finished both activities.

Carry the two baskets containing the suns, moons, stars, and planets **(Reproducible 8B, top)** to the table. Have the children come to the work table in groups of two or three. Give each child a small paper cup (not plastic or foam). Let each child tape two or three shapes (suns, moons, stars, or planets) to his or her cup in whatever pattern the child chooses. The shapes should not be right next to one another. Give each child a thick hand towel or dish towel to stuff inside the cup for padding. Show each child how to use a push pin or a sharpened pencil to punch the holes about a quarter-inch apart all along the edges of the shapes they have taped to the cup. The towel should keep the children from poking their fingers, but still caution the children to keep their hands away from the sharp ends of the push pins or pencils. You will want to supervise this activity closely.

When each child has punched out all the holes, have him or her remove the taped-on shapes. Make sure that all the push pins or pencils are collected when the children are finished with them. Have the children take turns using the **mini flashlight keychains**. Show the children how to hold a flashlight inside a cup so that the design lights up. Turn off the lights in the room to see the design better.

Supplies:
Reproducible 8B (top)
small paper cups
thick hand towels or dish towels
push pins or sharpened pencils
tape

Zillies®:
mini flashlight keychains
baskets

Squares and Stars

Photocopy the game grid **(page 172)**, enlarging it as much as possible.

Say: Let's play a game that's all about making squares. A square has four sides, right? That's four lines. Each of you will take a turn drawing a line between two dots anywhere on the page. Your lines can either go up and down or from side to side. If you can draw a line that finishes up a box, you can draw a star in that box. We'll play until the whole grid is covered with squares and stars.

The pattern is started in the top left-hand corner of the game grid. Younger children may need guidance until enough lines are drawn that a square has been completed. If stars are too complicated, let them draw an x instead.

Supplies:
page 172
markers
optional: chalkboard and chalk, or dry eras board and markers

Zillies®:
none

YOUNGER ELEMENTARY: LESSON 8

97

Bible Story

Sun, Moon, Stars, Planets

by Betsi H. Smith

Divide the children into four groups. Name one group "sun," another group "moon," the third group "stars," and the last group "planets." Have the children stand in a circle. Each group should stand together, with plenty of room between the groups, so children have room to move. Bring out the **zoo animal finger puppet**.

Have the puppet say: Hi there! Remember me? I'm *(puppet's name).* **Today you're going to help tell the story. You're in groups, right? I'm going to give each group a movement. Since the sun is so bright, I want those of you in the sun group to put your hands above your eyes, like you're blocking out the sunlight, and squint your eyes. Since the moon comes out at night, those of you in the moon group will put your hands together, put them beside your cheek, and close your eyes, like you're sleeping. Those of you in the star group, think about how many stars twinkle in the night sky. I'd like you to hold up your arms and open and close your fists really fast, like you're showing us a lot of twinkling stars. Since the planets turn around the sun, I want each person in the planet group to turn in a circle.** *(Have the children practice their group's motion.)* **Now listen carefully for the name of your group in the story. Whenever you hear it, do the motions we just talked about. This is going to be fun! Ready?** *(Set the puppet aside for now.)*

God created everything there is. God created the **sun**, and the **moon**, and the **stars**, and the **planets**.

The **sun** gives us light during the day. When we are cold, the **sun** warms our skin. When we are wet, the **sun** dries us off. Plants need the **sun** to grow. With a little help from the **sun**, a small seed can grow into a big oak tree. With a little help from the **sun**, a tiny seedling can grow into a tall sunflower.

Early in the morning, we can watch the **sun** rise. Late in the evening, we can watch the **sun** set. Sometimes, if it's cloudy, we can't see the **sun** at all. But it's there. The **sun** is very strong. We can burn our skin if we stay in the **sun** too long. We can hurt our eyes if we look directly at the **sun**.

God created the **sun**. God also created the **moon**, and the **stars**, and the **planets**.

The **moon** can be seen at night. Sometimes the **moon** makes a big circle in the sky. Sometimes the **moon** is just a half circle. Sometimes the **moon** is just a little sliver showing in the sky, and sometimes the **moon** doesn't show up at all. When the **moon** comes out, people know it's time to go to sleep. When the **moon** disappears and the **sun** comes out, people know it's time to wake up.

The **moon** isn't as big as the **sun** or as strong as the **sun**. It makes the night a little bit brighter, though. The **moon** can help guide your way if you're taking a nighttime walk with your parents or if you're chasing fireflies in your backyard. Some people used to say that the **moon** was made of cheese. That's not true. Some people used to say that a man lives in the **moon**. That's not true, either.

God created the **moon**. God also created the **sun**, and the **stars**, and the **planets**.

Look up at the sky at night, and you'll probably see lots and lots of lights. Those are **stars**. **Stars** look very, very small when we look at them from earth, but they're not small at all. They're just very, very far away. The brightest **stars** in our sky is the North Star. The North **Star** is so bright, ship captains used to look for it at night. The North **Star** helped keep them from getting lost.

For fun, some people study the **stars**. They can point out shapes in the **stars**, just like you can sometimes see shapes in clouds. They give names to these star shapes, like Big Dipper or Orion.

God created the **stars**. God also created the **sun**, and the **moon**, and the **planets**.

We live on a **planet** named Earth. It isn't the only **planet**, though. People who study the **planets** have found at least eight other **planets**. Some of the **planets** don't look anything like Earth. Mars looks red. Saturn looks like it has rings around it.

The **planets** are very far away. Sometimes you can see some of the **planets** when you look into the sky at night. But most of the time, you need a telescope to see the **planets**.

God created the **planets**. God also created the **sun**, and the **moon**, and the **stars**. God created everything there is.

Bring the puppet back out to talk to the children.

Have the puppet say: Wasn't that fun? You did a great job telling that story. I like to look at the stars at night. I'm glad that God created stars, and planets, and the sun, and the moon.

Have the puppet say goodbye until next week.

YOUNGER ELEMENTARY: LESSON 8

Bible ZONE

Choose one or more activities to immerse your children in the Bible story.

Supplies:
Bible
Reproducible 8B, bottom
paper, plastic, or foam cups
paper napkins
tape or rubber bands

Zillies®:
none

Punch and Play

Before class, cut apart one set of the Bible verse stars **(Reproducible 8B, bottom)** that you photocopied for an earlier activity. Put the stars inside the paper, plastic, or plastic foam cups, one star per cup. Lay a paper napkin over the top of each cup to cover the opening. Tighten the napkins around the cups with rubber bands.

Have a student hold the Bible open to Psalms. Show the children where today's verse is found in the Bible. **Say the Bible verse for the students: "I often think / of the heavens / your hands / have made, / and of the moon / and stars / you put / in place"** / (Psalm 8:3). Have them repeat it several times until they are familiar with it.

Give each child a cup. If you have more than nine children in your class, have some of the children work in pairs. If you have fewer than nine children, participate yourself or have some of the children take more than one cup.

Have each child punch through the napkin covering the top of the cup and take out the Bible verse star. Have the children arrange themselves so that the Bible verse is in order. If necessary, repeat the verse out loud as they work.

Supplies:
Creation pictures started last week
yellow markers, crayons, paint, or construction paper and glue
optional: see page 169

Zillies®:
none

Add to Creation

Give the children the Creation pictures that they started last week (or follow the instructions on page 169, if the children are making creation boxes).

Say: Today we talked about when God created . . . *(the sun, the moon, the stars, and the planets).* **Let's add the sun to our garden pictures.**

Let the children use a yellow marker or crayon or yellow paint to add a sun to their daytime pictures. Or cut circles from yellow construction paper for the children to glue in the sky. (Children this age often picture the sun with rays projecting from it. Let them create a sun however they choose.)

God made the sun, the moon, the stars, and the planets.

BibleZone® LIVE

Life Zone

Choose one or more activities to bring the Bible to life.

Sing and Celebrate

Have the children close their eyes and listen to the music of "Creation Dance" **(CD, Track 9)**. Lead the children in the suggested motions as you read the following. You may wish to practice saying the lines with the music before actually leading the children.

Creation Dance

In the beginning, there was nothing.
The universe was empty and had no shape.
(Have children get close to the ground and cover their heads.)
Then God said, "Let there be light!"
And the light appeared!
God saw that it was good.
(Have children uncover their heads and stand to move to the music.)
"But wait," God said. "What shall I do with the darkness? It is good, too!"
So God separated the light and the dark and called the dark, night.
(Have children close their eyes.)
Then in the night, God placed twinkling stars, shooting stars, and the big round moon!
And God saw that it was good!
(Have the children pretend to be twinkling stars, shooting stars, and big round moons.)
Evening passed and the morning came.
That was the end of the day.
God was very pleased with the creation.
God saw that it was good!

Words by Lora Jean Gowan. ©2000 Cokesbury.

Supplies:
CD player

Zillies®:
CD

YOUNGER ELEMENTARY: LESSON 8

Life Zone

Choose one or more activities to bring the Bible to life.

Supplies:
Reproducible 8B (bottom)
felt-tip markers
paper punch
scissors
chenille stems
drinking straws
optional: clear, self-adhesive paper

Zillies®:
tracing rulers

Bible Verse Bracelet

Cut the drinking straws into half-inch pieces. Cut enough to have eight pieces for each child. Give each child the eight pieces and a copy of the Bible verse stars (**Reproducible 8B, bottom**) that you photocopied earlier.

Let the children take turns using the stencils on the **tracing rulers** and felt-tip markers to draw designs on the back of the stars. The stars will be more durable if you help the children seal the stars in clear, self-adhesive paper. (The children should decorate the sheet of Bible verse stars first, then seal the sheet in self-adhesive paper, and then cut out the stars.) Have the children cut out the stars and use a paper punch to punch a hole in the top of each one.

Give each child a chenille stem. Show the children how to thread the Bible verse stars in order onto the chenille stem. Have them thread a star on first, then a piece of straw, continuing until all the pieces are on the chenille stem. Have the children fit their Bible verse bracelets around their wrists and twist the ends of the chenille together to fasten the bracelet closed.

Say: Your bracelet can remind you that God created the world.

Supplies:
Transparency 1
overhead projector
CD player

Zillies®:
CD

Closing Time

Play "Awesome God" (**CD, Track 8**) to signal that it is closing time. Review American Sign Language for the song (**Transparency 1**). Play the song again. Encourage the children to sign and sing along. **Say the Bible verse: "I often think of the heavens your hands have made, and of the moon and stars you put in place"** (Psalm 8:3). Have the children repeat it.

Say: We started talking about Creation last week. Who can remember what God created first? *(sky, water, land, plants)* What part of Creation did we talk about today? *(sun, moon, stars, planets)*

Pray: God, we love this beautiful world that you have created. Help us to remember to look up and appreciate the sun, the moon, the stars, and the planets. Thank you for loving us so much that you gave us this world in which we live. Amen.

Have the children take home their shine-through stars and Bible verse bracelets.

Give each child a copy of the HomeZone to take home to parents.